My Savior at My Side

My Savior at My Side

richard g. korthals

reflective

faith

stories

Cover illustration by Matthew Ambre.

Library of Congress Cataloging-in-Publication Data
Korthals, Richard G.
     My Savior at my side : reflective faith stories / Richard Korthals.
     p. cm.
     ISBN 0-570-05265-3
     1. Christian life—Anecdotes. 2. Christian life—Meditations.
     I. Title
     BV4501.3 .K67 2001
     242—dc21   2001002849

1 2 3 4 5 6 7 8 9 10   10 09 08 07 06 05 04 03 02 01

IT WAS THE SPRING OF 1945.
*My Savior, who had been at my side through the
ups and downs of my growing-up years, decided it
was time to assign a personal representative. His
guiding hand led me into the presence of a lovely
air evacuation nurse in the most unlikely of places.
The story of how He brought us together, with love
quickly blooming, forms the introduction to the
story "Little People."*

*Lynn has been at my side through all the
intervening years, not only as wife and mother of
our children, but also as friend and compassionate
companion. Her unwavering faith in our Savior
and unfailing love for me has been my inspiration.
It bolstered my desire to pen the stories that she
has heard so many times—that color the fabric
woven during years spent side-by-side.*

*I therefore dedicate this book to Lynn, the
woman who is still the love of my life, and to the
God who brought her to my side.*

Dick Korthals
Pentecost 2001

PREFACE

It is easy to feel secure in God's arms when things are going well. It is in the darker moments when we feel insecure, when we cry "Where are You, God?" Where do we find the assurance of God's presence and the strength for life's journey when everything around us seems to fail?

My first response is to open my Bible and let God's promises speak to my fears. Unfortunately, my frail human nature has a tendency to question and doubt. Deep inside there lurks a sinful desire for concrete evidence and proof that the Lord means what He says.

Our Heavenly Father recognizes that weakness in all of us. He tells us to "look to the past!" His promise to Joshua included an assurance, "As I was with Moses, so I will be with you; I will never leave you nor forsake you" (Joshua 1:5b). "When fears arise," God was saying, "think back and remember all I did for Moses. Rest assured that I will do the same for you." David's confidence in confronting Goliath was similarly rooted in history. "The Lord who delivered me from the paw of the lion and the paw of the bear will deliver me from the hand of this Philistine" (1 Samuel 17:37a). Recalling God's past victories gave David courage for the present.

Jesus dealt with the anxieties of His followers in yet another way. He advised them to observe creation and recall the Creator. "Look at the birds of the air; they do not sow or reap or store away in barns, and yet your heavenly Father feeds them. Are you not much more valuable than they? ... And why do you worry about clothes? See how the lilies of the field grow. They do not labor or spin. Yet I tell you that not even Solomon in all his splendor was dressed like one of these" (Matthew 6:26, 28–29). One way that Jesus taught us to see evidence of God's love is through the way He cares for all of His creation.

My Savior at My Side is a collection of personal stories drawn from both of these sources—the past and the present. It is therefore divided into two parts. The goal is to help you discover for yourself the inspiration and reassurance in both past and present.

The first half of the book is a collection of stories recounting specific times when, to paraphrase a popular illustration, "the two sets of footprints in the sand became one." It is in reviewing the past that I find a direction for the future. It helps me see my Savior as not only a friend who walks beside me, but also as the One who redeemed me and goes before me to show me the way and bring me His peace.

The second half of the book consists of stories about nature. How comforting to "look at the birds of the air." The antics of a saucy chickadee are enough to brighten the gloomiest of days. The carefree attitude it displays while braving the worst of winter weather gives evidence of an instinctive trust in the Creator to provide. The instinct is also seen in the sacrificial care displayed by a mother mouse in search of its offspring or the struggle of a wasp to provide food for larva that will emerge from its eggs.

The observance of creatures great and small and the world they inhabit gives evidence to the power of God as set forth in Genesis and framed in the song of the psalmist. Rooted in Scripture, we hear God's power in echoing thunder, see it in mountain grandeur, and feel it in the gentle breeze. Unfortunately, our sinful, shortsighted nature causes us to misinterpret this divine power. Some need the reassurance that God's power will be applied with a loving hand. Millions of people feel they must earn His kindness. According to their belief systems, favorable treatment is obtained by appeasing Him by offering sacrifices or accomplishing tasks.

How different is the one true God who reveals Himself in Holy Scripture. There we learn that it was our God who sacrificed Himself on our behalf and that He freely loves us, irrespective of our status in life. His self-less concern for our eternal welfare is consistent year after year. It never changes.

It is only when I view the past through the cross of Christ that I see a loving God at work in my life. He is not only "out there," a powerful force who's "got the whole wide world in His hands." He is also in here with me every second of every minute of every day, showering me with grace and forgiveness and using His loving wisdom to guide my thoughts and direct my actions. How do I know this to be true? By clinging to the promises of my heavenly Father that are mine through faith in Christ. As I listen to His Word, dine at His Table, and recall my Baptism, I see God at work in my life.

It is my prayer that, through the Holy Spirit, the stories of *My Savior at My Side* will inspire reflections on your faith and bring forth new realizations in your life.

Dick Korthals

CONTENTS

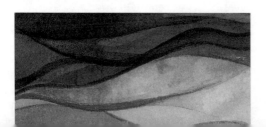

BROKEN TOYS

The pinnacle of age where I presently reside offers a vantage point from which to contemplate the twists and turns my life has taken. Most were slight changes in direction that seemed important at the time but had little lasting impact. There was an occasional major fork in the road, however, that evoked both agonizing pre-decisions and painful post-appraisals. My retirement from the United States Air Force and subsequent move to Concordia Lutheran Junior College at Ann Arbor, Michigan, fell into the latter category.

The job offer and contract that had arrived that spring brought the exciting possibility of a career change. It would fulfill my long-held dream of serving the Lord as a church worker, initially as a college professor and later, I thought, as a pastor. The summer overflowed with eager anticipation and tearful good-byes and culminated in an August 1 retirement ceremony. It marked the end of a "blue suit" career during which a Wisconsin farm boy had been transformed into a seasoned pilot, space engineer, and Air Force Academy professor. No longer would I be teaching cadets the intricacies of taking man to the moon. My emphasis now would be on helping people find their way to the cross.

We arrived in Ann Arbor on August 15. Our first disappointment came as we drove to the site of our new home. It had been purchased in April as a set of blueprints with a promised completion date of August 1, but the scrap-filled interior indicated the move-in date was still weeks away. We spent the next month sleeping on hospital beds in the college infirmary with our clothes and household goods packed in a warehouse.

That inconvenience proved minor, however, when compared to the shock I encountered when classes began in early September. The transition was similar to the shock experienced by the unprepared when entering a foreign culture.

My final year in the Air Force had been spent as head of the astronautics department. Perks included a personal secretary, designated parking space, and lunch in the Dean of Faculty dining room. My teaching load consisted of one section of a course that met three times weekly, with the course director preparing all lesson plans and exams. Cadets sprang to attention when I entered the room and addressed me as "Sir" or "Colonel."

Now, added to the unfamiliarity of having to scramble for a parking space was getting the attention of students when entering a classroom. The three weekly classroom hours of the previous year had been multiplied by six! Daily lesson plans were required for the three courses I was teaching for the first time. In addition, tests had to be written, typed (how I missed my secretary), duplicated, and graded. The assigning of grades, computerized at the Academy, now became my sole (and agonizing) responsibility. By the end of October, physical and mental exhaustion became a way of life.

Three of our four children experienced problems in adjusting. They had been transported from a semi-cloistered Air Force Academy community to the maelstrom of our college community. A daughter who would have been surrounded by devoted friends at family-oriented AFA high school felt lost and alone as one of 2,000 seniors with whom she had little in common. A son educated within the friendly confines of a small parochial school was ridiculed as the "The Bible Kid" at a public middle school because he carried a Bible to a weekly confirmation class. Another daughter who had left behind a treasured horse and the companionship of a fellow rider sought in vain for a similar experience in our new urban setting.

Late fall brought with it an endless stretch of leaden

skies and chilling drizzles that further dampened our spirits. The yard surrounding our new home was transformed into a sea of mud that had an irresistible attraction toward passing shoes. My wife, who abhors a dirty dwelling, fought a losing battle in her valiant efforts to keep floors clean.

It seemed like every day brought with it a new problem that had an impact on our family. Our thoughts naturally drifted back to the endless blue skies and warm sense of community left behind in Colorado. At the same time, a nagging question began to raise its ugly head. Was my decision to retire from the Air Force and move to Ann Arbor in accordance with God's will and a result of His prompting—or had my selfish desires played the dominant role?

In mid-December the college campus was transformed into a beehive of activity when students exchanged hugs and best wishes, packed their belongings in waiting automobiles, and went on Christmas vacation with loved ones. I breathed a sigh of relief in anticipation of a relaxed schedule and time for my family.

A bone-chilling drizzle was falling one Wednesday noon as I drove to the campus to complete some required paperwork. Sitting on the seat beside me was Jacque, our black miniature poodle celebrating his second year as a member of our family. I carried him as I walked to the administration building, and then let him sit at my feet as I accomplished the necessary task.

Busy with what I was doing, I failed to notice Jacque walk to a door to the adjacent cafeteria. Neither did I see an employee approach the entrance, open the door, and then let it slam shut—with the dog on the outside. By the time I got there, my tiny canine friend was racing across a bridge leading to a nearby orchard. He was probably paralyzed by fear and responded to a single overpowering instinct—to let his pint-sized legs propel him as fast and as far as possible. My running and calling only added to his confusion, and he soon disappeared in the tall grass.

I spent the next hour walking a crisscross pattern through the small grove of fruit trees bordering the campus. I could envision him cowering in his hiding place, trembling in the grip of unfounded terror. Softly calling his name again and again brought no response. It soon became apparent that the search would have to be extended.

A quick trip home resulted in three teenagers coming to help. Knee-high grass hampered our efforts as we anxiously tried to establish contact with our frightened friend. But by mid-afternoon it was obvious that little was being accomplished. Low hanging clouds added to the gloom of aching hearts as we returned home.

It was dusk when I decided to return for one last

desperate attempt. As I approached the orchard, the glare of headlights bouncing off the damp road briefly illuminated a tiny mound in the opposite lane. My worst fears were confirmed. It was the battered and torn body of our Jacque that I gently wrapped in a towel and placed in the trunk of the car.

My family cried when I shared the news of my discovery with them. A mental image of his lonely terror-filled final moments filled our minds and broke our hearts. It appeared to be a fitting culmination to the months of extreme disappointments and bitter frustrations we all shared.

The pain was quickly transformed into a bubbling cauldron of self-pity. I was angry as I saw myself abandoned by the God I was trying to serve. Had He been listening when I requested His help last spring while deciding which fork in the road to follow? Did He persuade me to follow a path filled with pitfalls and blind alleys so He could find amusement in my antics? Was this my reward for leaving a promising military career?

It was force of habit that prompted me to attend the final Advent service that evening. Even the prospect of hearing a message from my friend Eugene Krentz failed to penetrate the gloom that enveloped me. I settled in my pew determined to resist a God who I perceived as being cold and distant.

Gene's theme was "Broken Toys." His text was Isaiah 61:1, "The Spirit of the Sovereign LORD is on me, because the LORD has anointed me to preach good news to the poor. He has sent me to bind up the brokenhearted, to proclaim freedom for the captives and release from darkness for the prisoners."

He began his sermon by sharing Christmas memories from his childhood years during the Depression. Toys were few and far between and his parents scrimped and saved to be able to place them beneath the tree. These quickly became treasured possessions and were handled with great care. However, before long the inevitable would happen: a mishap would result in a broken toy.

He told of gathering up the pieces and running to his father with tears streaming down his face. His dad would wrap his arms around him and dry his tears. Then his skillful fingers would patiently repair and reassemble the shattered parts into a toy that was as good as new.

How similar that had been to my own childhood experience with a dad who was an expert at mending toys. Therefore, Gene's comparison between his earthly dad and our heavenly Father was easy for me to follow. As he spoke, I found my perception of a cold and distant God slowly fading from view. Instead I saw, shining through the gloom, a vision of my Father coming toward me with outstretched arms. In the quiet of that evening hour I let those arms enfold me as I placed the broken pieces of my life into His loving hands.

The memory of the peace and joy that flooded me will never leave me. Tears are welling up in my eyes as I write these words and recall that moment. How many others were present that night undergoing a similar struggle will never be known. However, there is one thing I do know. It was a loving God who understood my anger and shared my pain, a God so concerned for my well-being that He used a caring pastor to communicate an anecdote and relate it to Scripture in such a way that it changed my life forever.

That evening marked a turning point in my outlook. The problems were still there. In fact, some intensified. What had been added was the sure knowledge that my Savior was at my side—the same Savior who had opened His arms on the cross was waiting with open caring hands to gently take my broken toys and make them whole. It gave me a sense of joy, peace, and confidence that is still my most prized possession.

Broken Toys

When I was just a little boy
On our Wisconsin farm,
Dad's income, it was mighty low,

With five to feed and warm.
At Christmastime my mom would hunt
Through catalogs to find
Gifts she felt would meet the needs
For three lads on her mind.
Encased in Sears-brown, these would lie
Beneath the tree that morn,
Amidst the clothes a toy for each—
They almost looked forlorn.

But to our eyes how precious
For treasures we could see,
In unison we shouted,
"Look what they gave to me!"
Two cousins soon would join us,
And we five spent that day
In rough-and-tumble kinds of things
That boys do when they play.
Before long it would happen—
My toy would fly apart,
The tears of anguish that I shed
Bespoke a fractured heart.

Ravaged plaything clutched in breast
With sobs from depth of soul,
"Dad, fix my broken toy," I'd cry,
"Please, Daddy, make it whole."
He'd gently grasp in calloused hands

Those pieces I could find—
And ragged edges soon were joined
With naught but glue to bind.
Miraculous—it seemed to me
From my young point of view,
That he could take a broken toy,
And make it good as new!

Today I'm much, much older—
With toys no longer play—
Now I find that a broken life
More often comes my way.
Instead of toys, it's long-held dreams
For me that come apart,
And in place of twisted metal
Oft is found a shattered heart.
But tears of anguish have not changed,
Nor has my mournful cry—
Only now my heavenly Father's arms
Are the ones to which I fly.

"Dear God," I cry, "To You I give
This life so flawed and torn,
Oh Father, could You make it whole—
As first when I was born?"
"Of course, My son." His whispered voice
Comes gently to my ear,

"Give Me those bits and pieces
And new they shall appear."
With wondering eye I watch and see
Each jagged edge made plane
Then coated with the blood of Christ,
Are joined as one again.

In bonds of love the whole is wrapped
And, taking up a brush,
His pardon coats in lavish strokes
That hide what made me blush.
Oh, miracle of miracles!
What once in fragments lay
His loving fingers have made whole—
I'm born anew each day!
Because of Him I can again
Live days of peace and joy,
A Father who I now love more
Than when I was a boy.

He has sent me to bind up the brokenhearted, to pro-claim freedom for the captives and release from darkness for the prisoners. Isaiah 61:1

ALL IN DUE TIME

We purchased the home with one thought in mind. *This was it!* Our dream home, the one in which we intended to spend the remainder of our earthly pilgrimage. The tension of buying and selling, coupled with the turmoil of packing and unpacking, was now part of a never-to-be-repeated past. Historic Trinity Church had acquired two new members and their beautifully situated Pilgrim Cemetery two future residents.

All the right ingredients were in place. Two sets of children and grandchildren met the 50-mile-radius criteria. They were close, but not too close. The small town setting reminded us of our childhood, and people who understood and accepted us inhabited it. This was our town.

The one-and-a-half story gabled white brick home had two fireplaces and a wood-burning stove. There were also limitless opportunities to indulge in my passion for nature. The ancient beech and maple forest that adjoined our backyard was threaded by dozens of trails tailor-made for exploration by an eager hiker and his inquisitive canine companion. Nearby was a pristine Lake Michigan shoreline and thundering surf. We waited eagerly to embrace family members gathered at our home.

Events of the next 15 years strengthened our resolve to stay there. Interior and exterior remodeling and restoration enhanced "Grandma and Grandpa's house." Walls echoed with the laughter of our grandchildren and floors vibrated with their pounding feet. The house seemed destined to be ours forever.

A journey to Colorado Springs one spring began as an innocuous attempt to achieve twin goals. My primary purpose was participation in a reunion of Air Force pilots I had graduated with. The other goal was the renewing of friendships formed while stationed in that scenic city many years before. Interwoven was subtle arm-twisting to abandon the Midwest and return to the mountains. Our parting promise was, "We might consider it if you find the perfect house with the perfect view."

Two months later an excited friend called to inform us that the mission had been accomplished. Pictures quickly followed that verified her claim. Situated on a ridge with a commanding view extending from Pikes

Peak to the eastern plains, the house met real estate's defining "location, location, location" criteria. I lost my heart during a personal inspection several weeks later and discovered the potential for fulfilling a long-held dream: It presented a unique opportunity to finally have an office with a panoramic vista that could inspire literary endeavors. (By sheer coincidence the address was Inspiration Drive.)

The final piece of the puzzle seemed to fall into place when the local pastor expressed an immediate need for skills I was eager to provide. We placed "Grandma and Grandpa's house" in the hands of a realtor in September and signed the "Inspiration" contract two weeks later. In the meantime, letters were sent to the half-dozen individuals who at one time or another had begged to be "first in line" should we decide to sell our home. We were ready to contact a moving company and start packing!

The first indication that things would not go smoothly was when five of the six letters were returned with the comment, "We are not ready. Write again in 10 years if the house is still available." The remaining party had the financial means and desire for immediate purchase—with one proviso. They wanted the board of directors of the family camp bordering our property to grant them full access to the facilities. The blunt denial of their request brought our negotiations to an abrupt conclusion. With that came the depressing realization that the rapidly approaching winter season would end our dreams of a quick and easy sale.

It was while seeking an outlet for my mounting frustration that thoughts turned to the plight of our daughter, a single mom who lived 50 miles away. Her tiny two-bedroom house was bulging at the seams. The need for expansion had long been apparent. It was the "how" that was elusive.

Now an unexpected bundle of free time stimulated creativity. The "how" vision became reality one October morning and within days had been translated into an elementary blueprint for an addition. A contract was signed with a local builder in early November, with the stipulation that I would be permitted to undertake certain projects. A cold and wet Thanksgiving weekend was spent tearing shingles from a breezeway roof and carting the debris to a Dumpster.

With each day another piece of the dream became reality, and by Christmas the addition had been fully enclosed. Sanding and staining became the new orders of the day (and evening) as Lynn and I prepared trim for the contractor's finishing touches. Crucial decisions were made daily, with the major burden of responsibility falling on my shoulders. A daughter occupied with maintaining house and home found neither time nor energy for the task. When the contractor submitted his final bill a few weeks later, there were still dozens of projects awaiting completion.

This was also the time of a prolonged struggle with God. "Why," I pleaded, "did I have the opportunity for meaningful service only to have it yanked away by not being able to sell our home? Is it really my purpose at this point in my life to paint boards and pound nails when I could be helping others find their way to Christ? Can't You see my anxiety and feel my frustration? What are You doing to me, God? Have You forgotten that I exist?" The margin of the Bible I was reading at the time is filled with notations expressing gloom and despair. Yet twinkling in the darkness is an occasional ray of hope or encouragement discovered in God's message to me on that day.

Our moods brightened as the days lengthened and a flower-strewn carpet of spring replaced the well-worn browns and grays of winter. Our area was a Mecca for tourists and each bursting leaf and rising flower brought with it new dreams of hordes of buyers. We spent days ensuring that every element in our spacious yard was pleasing to the eye. Our adrenaline surged every time the phone rang and our pulse pounded when a passing auto slowed to a crawl. All to no avail. The crowd of curiosity seekers came, looked, and left. We received only two offers, both too low.

We made three decisions as summer merged into

autumn. First, we would take the house off the market at the end of a year and allow it to "rest." Second, we would remove one element of uncertainty by moving to Colorado at the end of November. Third, we would devote our full energies to finishing the remaining projects at our daughter's home.

Lynn and I checked off the home-improvement projects one by one. Walls painted and papered, floor sanded and finished, garage storage completed, blinds hung, entry porch and deck built, exterior painted—the list went on. It was mid October before the final project loomed. I spent the last week building a small utility room off the kitchen. Our labor of love was finally completed and my heart sang.

Two days later I was working in my upstairs office when the phone rang. It was our real estate agent asking if we would like to show our home to a young couple who had just dropped by his office. I gave him a half-hearted "yes."

I watched from the window as they arrived 10 minutes later. Their apparent youth convinced me that this was another "Lookie! Oooo!" couple. I remained at my desk for the next half-hour while tracking their progress through the house via the sound of their voices. "This is taking more time than I expected," I thought as footsteps could be heard on the stairs. "I wonder what is arousing their interest?"

That question was answered 30 minutes later when the young man introduced himself and then proceeded to describe the financial bonanza they had encountered the past year. "You may be wondering why I am telling you this," he said. "I want you to be aware of our financial condition because my wife has fallen in love with your home and we are going to buy it!" The words we had longed to hear for 14 months fell on unbelieving ears. The disappointments of the prior year were finally erased by the binding contract we signed the following day. Our long wait had ended at a moment when my hope had vanished.

Our daughter and her family joined us that weekend as we celebrated our good fortune and praised God for His blessing. We gathered Saturday evening to share the warmth of family love and revel in the excitement of the future. It was during a lull in the conversation that our daughter suddenly said, "Mom and Dad, I was devastated when you first told me of your move because I thought you were leaving to get away from me and my problems. But the many ways in which you demonstrated your love during the past year have convinced me otherwise."

The tears that filled my eyes dissolved the scales that had been distorting my vision of God. He who I had begun to see as a disinterested observer had instead been deeply involved in every event along the way. As I mentally knelt before Him that evening, I could almost hear Him say; "My son, I felt your frustration and tasted the bitterness of your disappointments. I heard your prayer for a favorable decision that first September and I could have enabled an immediate sale. But I also saw a grieving daughter, and My concern for her well-being superceded the desires of your heart. I have been aware of your dreams and they will now be fulfilled—at a time of My choosing."

I will never forget the humbling demonstration of God's love revealed to me through the shared thoughts of a dear daughter, nor the deep and abiding peace that followed. God loves me! He does care! He told me so! But He also cares for those around me in ways that I will never understand. Why am I so certain? Because of His unfailing promises to me.

It Seems So Simple

*It seems so simple—a house is found in
distant city cast,*

*That inner fancy strikes,
and for which
purchase soon is made.*

*The ideal home, a peaceful haven for
decade or two just past*

*Is given into younger hands with dreams
of future newly laid.*

*Forgotten in that moment are the
friendships that we glean*

*From deep within the crucible of joys and
sorrows shared.*

*The links of love that twist and bend as
distance grows between,*

*Cause tearful pain as parting comes from
those for whom we cared.*

It's not as simple as it seems.

*It seems so simple—a yellow-pages call
that's free of toll*

*Brings forth a reassuring voice dispelling
fear of future day.*

*"You're in good hands!" speaks comfort to
an apprehensive soul*

*While painting scenes of household goods
already underway.*

*Forgotten in that moment are the shelters
filled to overflow*

*With piece and parcel, each by far too
precious to disdain,*

*Awaiting padded comfort in containers
soon stacked row on row*

*By wife and mate with tiring bodies
touched by agony of pain.*

It's not as simple as it seems.

It seems so simple—to hear of shepherds'
awe and angel songs,

Of birth in manger bare, devoid of all
that comfort makes.

A tiny babe so helpless, and on mother's
arm He now belongs

While from her loving breast His daily
sustenance partakes.

Forgotten in that moment is a Father's
glory willingly foregone

So that our human nature He might take
as though it were His own,

And died a tortuous death in which for
all our sins He did atone.

It's not as simple as it seems.

It seems so simple—to let this Christ as
Savior enter in,

With arms of faith to grasp His gift of
love so freely given—

The pardon purchased for each person
waiting to be freed of sin,

A living Lord within us now, with us eter-
nally in heaven.

And that is as simple as it seems.

"For My thoughts are not your thoughts, neither are your ways My ways," declares the Lord. *"As the heavens are higher than the earth, so are My ways higher than your ways and My thoughts higher than your thoughts."* Isaiah 55:8–9

And we know that in all things God works for the good of those who love Him, who have been called according to His purpose. Romans 8:28

CLIMBING QUANDARY

I know it may sound strange, but I have had this crazy desire to climb a Fourteen'er for years. Every spring brings the same resolve, and each fall finds the goal remaining unfulfilled. Sometimes it has been lack of time or climbing companions, but most often the restraint has been fear of the unknown. Would I be able to muster sufficient physical endurance to complete the climb in that rarefied atmosphere? Would the trails be easy to find and follow, or would I have to make my own? Excuses piled up as one question seemed to generate another.

All this came to an end one summer when the opportunity to satisfy that daft yearning became reality. Lynn and I celebrated our wedding anniversary by inviting our children and grandchildren to join us for a week at a guest ranch in Colorado. Intertwined in the days of family, fun, and food were a variety of planned activities including horseback riding, rafting, and hiking for those wishing to participate. Scheduled for Friday was a climb to the top of 14,265-foot Mount Quandary. Sherry, Patti, and David decided this would be the ideal way to help me celebrate my 73rd birthday.

Twelve intrepid climbers huddled around our fearless leader in the pre-dawn chill. Excitement crackled in the air as John gave us our final instructions before embarking on the 20-mile drive to the trailhead. It was an hour later, with the sun barely cracking the horizon, when we shouldered our packs and were on our way. At 11,000 feet we were still below the tree line. Ahead of us lay a well-defined path snaking upward through the pines.

The unrelenting pace John set at first had a dual purpose. First, he wanted to get us up to and off of the top of the mountain before noontime thunderstorms formed. Second, the poorly conditioned and weak at heart needed quick deterrent. My test was coming early! However, imagine my surprise when 15 minutes later I found myself near the head of the pack! "It's only three and a half miles to the top, and I am acclimated to high altitude," I said to myself. "I'll show these flatlanders!"

An hour later I was regretting that brash self-assessment of my abilities. The "legs go first" truism had become reality. "Fatigue" took on an entirely new meaning with an intensity I had never previously experienced.

The 26 years that separated me from the next oldest member of the group were taking their toll. Legs rebelled when asked to raise leaden feet over the next rock. Lungs struggled to absorb oxygen from the thin air. Any lull seemed like paradise.

The mental struggle was even more intense than the physical. Staring ahead, I saw the rock and snowfields covering the steep slopes separating me from the summit. At that moment an inner voice began saying, "You're stupid to submit your body to this punishment! Quit now before you have a heart attack. The others will understand. They all realize you're much older."

The encouraging words of two daughters and a son and the dream of an easy descent kept me struggling upward. Each rock became an accomplishment, every ridge a victory to celebrate. A final burst of adrenaline provided the energy necessary to kick toeholds in the snow-covered slope to the summit. Waiting to greet "the old goat's" arrival with a cheer were the eight other climbers.

A blazing mid-day sun warmed our bodies as we gathered photographic evidence of our accomplishment. The spectacular vista punctuated by the spiny backbone dividing our nation's watershed overwhelmed our senses and made our mountain-top lunch an unforgettable experience. The brief respite was sufficient to "recharge my battery" for the eagerly anticipated return trip. After all, it was all downhill from here. What could be easier!

Moments later the icy slope of the snowfield shattered the "easier downhill" hypothesis. Losing a toehold on the uphill climb would have meant a short face-forward fall. Slipping on descent meant a backward tumble and a swift snowy slide to the rocks below. Pulse-pounding apprehension replaced happy anticipation as I realized that severe bodily injury was a distinct possibility.

Legs drained of energy by the morning's exertion now ached with weariness as a new set of muscles came into play. A trail so easily detected on the upward journey now disappeared from view when seen from a different perspective. Rocks that appeared solid under slowly applied foot-pressure when climbing now threatened to execute an ankle-breaking roll when struck by the hard thrust of a downward stride. The metal hiking staff, once looked upon as an extravagant and dangerous lightning rod, now became an absolute necessity.

The excitement felt earlier in the day vanished as three offspring and I found ourselves left behind by the other climbers eager to return to the comfort of the ranch. One dream dominated as trail-worn feet took us back to the car parked at the trailhead. It was of a whirlpool tub waiting to gently warm and massage dozens of throbbing muscles and 10 aching toes.

The memory of that climb and the lessons I learned will always be with me. Above all it taught me to appreciate the close correlation between the physical test I experienced that day and my walk through life—as difficult as the upward climb may be, it is the descent into the valley that tries one's spirit.

Acquiring an education, finding that special person, establishing a home, raising a family, pursuing a fulfilling career—those experiences are all part of the climb. We may suffer from fatigue, but there is also a sense of exhilaration as we look ahead with anticipation. Friends and family are there to lend a helping hand and cheer us on as we struggle along paths and conquer summits along the way.

How different when we descend into the valley. There is no excitement in illness, no anticipation in the death of a loved one, no thrill in the loss of a job. Body and mind, already weary from life's journey, rebel at the added pain. Even close friends may abandon us as goals disappear and the path becomes obscure.

Yet I know that in the darkest of moments my Savior will be at my side. He will be there to match my stumbling steps with His firm stride while He holds my hand in His warm and tender grasp. With David I can confidently say, "*The* LORD *is* my *shepherd. ...* Even though I walk through the valley of the shadow of death, I will fear no evil, for *You* are with me; *Your* rod and *Your* staff, they comfort me" (Psalm 23:1–4).

In that promise I find my hope and strength. In that Jesus I find the joy that fills life to overflowing. It is in that Christ, whose birth we celebrate, whose death we remember, and whose resurrection we share that we place our trust and find our peace. That holds true, even when the path leads to a downward descent.

FEAR NOT

The ending of the Cold War was sudden, spectacular, and surprising. The images of East and West Germans pouring through the openings hammered in the Berlin Wall are still vivid. But rapidly fading are recollections of the shroud of potential nuclear destruction that enveloped our nation for 40 years.

Bomb shelters fully equipped for long-term survival were a feature in many American homes. Elementary school children rehearsed nuclear blast survival techniques by huddling beneath their desks.

Adding to our citizens' fear was a made-for-TV movie titled "The Day After." It was a powerful drama portraying with stark realism the catastrophic aftermath of a nuclear confrontation. Depicted in graphic detail was the devastating destruction resulting from the detonation of a hydrogen bomb above a small city in Kansas.

The horror began with a blinding flash that filled

the TV screen. Milliseconds later, the movie showed a shock wave of superheated gas that first toppled and then burned to a crisp everything in its path. A signature mushroom cloud that followed rained deadly radioactive particles over all that remained. Days of suffering preceded the inevitable death awaiting those who had been exposed. The struggle for survival of the remaining remnant provided the drama justifying the title "The Day After."

During the Cold War, international tension between the major powers became an accepted way of life. Satellites prowled space 24 hours a day with electronic eyes searching for the telltale plume of a missile launch. The chairs occupied by military crews poised to launch retaliatory strikes from underground silos were never empty.

Where was God in all of this? Had He lost control of the affairs of nations or was He just playing games? These and similar questions not only burned within the hearts of many Christians during those trying times, they remain with us today. What proof do we have that God is aware of our predicament and is concerned about our welfare?

The doubts and fears experienced during the uncertainty of the Cold War are repeated day after day in a multitude of situations. A body harboring a deadly disease, financial ruin, break-up of a family, death of a loved one—each in its own way triggers questions concerning the presence of God and His love for us.

Is it possible to find peace and hope in our unstable world? The human mind may unlock the doors of peace among nations but it will never be capable of fully grasping God's love for us. Only God the Holy Spirit can do that. The answers to our anxious questions are inscribed on the sacred pages of God's Word. In Scripture we learn of the divine love that was visibly demonstrated in a dusty stall and in Christ's saving act on a darkened hillside. And we come to the Lord's Table to be refreshed in His unconditional love for us. The poem that follows may help you understand why:

Fear Not

> *A blinding flash of light,*
> *a ravenous globe of searing flame*
> *Rolls endlessly across a Kansas plain,*
> *leaving in its wake*
> *The half-digested scraps of seared corpse*
> *and twisted frame.*
> *Our mind rebels,*
> *and from within there wells a rising tide*
> *of fear.*
> *"Where is God?" we cry. "Where is He,*
> *the one who said that at His Word*
> *The stars were set upon their course,*

who holds the sun and moon
Within the palm of His almighty hand?
Can He no longer guide
The deeds and destiny of these, the work
of that creating Word?
Has He forgotten me?"

A bruising stab of pain engulfs our senses
as we lie breathless
Waiting for the next onslaught to come.
Our mind and body,
Wracked and torn by endless strife with
this relentless foe,
Cries out at thought of all that once was
ours, but now seems lost.
"Why me, O God?" we cry. "Why does
He let me struggle on and on
When once His Son reached out His
hand and at His touch
The blind could see, the lame could walk,
and even lepers—
Above all most afflicted—saw ravaged
bodies once again made whole.
Has He forgotten me?"

A bursting bubble of glistening dreams
spatters o'er our being,
Engulfing us in bitter dregs of fears made

real and hopes awry.

A future seemingly assured by that which
was most cherished,

Our means of livelihood—a spouse—
a home—have vanished,

Leaving us immersed in swirling depths of
loneliness and doubt.

"Where are You, God?" we cry. "Why has
He snatched away from me

All that once made my life complete?
Cannot He who long ago

Sent us a Son who wept in sorrow
and uplifted the downtrodden,

See within my aching breast a shattered
and despairing heart?

Has He forgotten me?"

A brilliance flashes o'er the darkened hills
and, reaching down,

Envelops prostrate forms of cowering
shepherds on a field below.

"Fear not!" the words that calmed their
dread remain undimmed,

As clear and ringing now as once they
were those centuries ago.

"Fear not!" the angels herald. "Your
Savior has been born."

"Fear not! I will be with you," vows
Christ our Living Lord.

"Fear not!" our Father reassures us,
"I know each sparrow.

And you, so much more precious, are also
in My loving hands.

Forgotten by Him who knows and loves
me—as He does you?"

Fear not!

God is our refuge and strength, an ever-present help in trouble. Therefore we will not fear, though the earth give way and the mountains fall into the sea. Psalm 46:1–2

What, then, shall we say in response to this? If God is for us, who can be against us? He who did not spare His own Son, but gave Him up for us all—how will He not also, along with Him, graciously give us all things? Romans 8:31–32

FIX YOUR EYES

David cupped his hand over the telephone receiver as he turned to me and said, "Dad, it's Dennis. He would like to have you join him for an hour of aerobatics!"

Aerobatics! The mere thought sent a tingle of excitement, mingled with stomach-churning apprehension, coursing through my body. Thirty-five years of physical deterioration were separating me from the last time I had strapped myself into a T-bird and "flung my eager craft through footless halls of air." G-forces were then encountered on a regular basis with inner-ear balance organs still possessing their youthful vigor. But what about now? Was the ignominy of filling a burp-bag in my immediate future? A dozen thoughts raced through my mind in the two seconds before I said, "Tell him we'll be there!"

The concrete arteries that connected our home to the airfield were clogged. Snail-like progress gave me adequate opportunity to repeat the refrain "I *will not* get airsick!" dozens of times. We finally stopped before a small hangar housing an immaculate yellow open-cockpit bi-plane. Dennis greeted us and then introduced me to his pride and joy, a Great Lakes stunt plane modeled after the famous WWII Stearman. I could hardly contain my excitement as, reaching back into the halls of memory, I found myself automatically adjusting the seat-pack parachute while pulling on the leather helmet and goggles. Never in my wildest dreams had the possibility of again experiencing the thrill of "head-in-the-slipstream" flying entered my mind.

Sliding into the narrow open cockpit, then adjusting and fastening seat belt and shoulder harness—how quickly the years vanished. As we taxied to the end of the runway, I could almost hear my instructor's voice barking at me through the Gosport tubes. The familiar magneto check, an okay from the tower followed by a burst of power, and we were airborne. A gentle left turn placed us on a climbing course to our maneuver area. A chill nipped at cheeks and slipped behind a loose-fitting jacket. My thoughts slipped back to late fall mornings in Oklahoma and the welcome warmth of the bulky sheepskin jackets and helmets we wore.

After two clearing turns Dennis' voice over the intercom snapped me back to the present, "Are you ready for a barrel roll?" "Let her rip!" was my response, filled with all the bravado I could muster. Forces momentarily thrust me against the side of the cockpit, yet kept me pinned against the seat in a perfectly executed roll. Miracle of miracles, my stomach remained stable. I had remembered an old adage, "Keep your eyes fixed on a reference point," and it had worked.

Another barrel roll was followed by several loops, and in each the jolt of prop wash at completion assigned the grade of 100 percent for piloting skills. Eight point rolls, hammerhead stalls, Immelmanns, Cuban eights—we did them all! Forces tugged and pushed on my body, but my eyes remained clear and my stomach at rest. In each case, despite all the twists and turns the maneuvers required, my focus had remained fixed on that magic reference point located directly over the nose. I felt like doing a victory roll!

Dennis had told me in advance that the four-leaf clover, because of the loss of altitude, would be our final maneuver. We would do four loops in succession, with a 90-degree roll on each descent changing the direction of the next loop. It sounded like a simple repeat of what we had done earlier, but by the time we had completed the second loop my stomach was shouting a different story. The crescendo of churning that was convulsing my innards midway through loop number three was a prelude to the major battle within by the time the final loop was completed.

Never have the words, "Let's head for home!" sounded so welcome! Yet even in level flight the refrain I clung to was being replaced by a desire to grab the burp-bag. My brow bathed in cold sweat attested to the intensity of the struggle. Huge gulps of fresh air—and a jolt of pride—finally attained the victory, but it was by the narrowest of margins.

What had made the difference? In retrospect I realized that during the previous series of maneuvers it had been possible to fix my eyes on a point either straight ahead or directly over the aircraft. I had forgotten that, because of the 90-degree roll between each loop of the four-leaf clover, the focal point on the horizon must be located by looking past the wingtip rather than over the nose. My balance organs were protesting via my stomach because I had lost the point of reference.

There have been times in my life when an emotional "four-leaf clover" suddenly interrupted the normal flow of daily "maneuvers," leaving me with emotions in turmoil. The sudden and unexpected death of my precious mom, uncertainties about my children as they struggled toward maturity, a job that turned sour and left me distressed—each caused me to become emotionally disoriented. Grasping for stability, I instinctively turned to familiar "over the nose" reference points: my wife, relatives, friends, or material possessions. But the drastic and unforeseen 90-degree turns were too much to conquer. The "burp-bag" appeared inevitable.

Then one day I opened my Bible and found, in Hebrews 12:2, the solution. "Let us fix our eyes on Jesus, the Author and Perfecter of our faith," was God's message to me. "You are looking in the wrong direction," He seemed to be saying. I saw, in the midst of all the twists and turns of my life, the constant presence of Jesus. As I riveted my gaze on Him, I saw the cross and felt the warmth of His love surround me. And in Him I found the inner peace that I craved.

In addition to being beside me, He is also in that other "cockpit" with His hands firmly on the controls, guiding me through all the "four-leaf clovers" encountered in life. And someday I will hear from Him that welcome message, "Let's head for home!" As He turns toward heaven, an eternity of smooth flying will lie ahead.

FREE AT LAST

I will always remember the gala celebrations that were part and parcel of our nation's 200th birthday celebration. Patriotic displays recalling our heritage were held throughout the land. Every day seemed to bring a new outburst of national fervor.

Lynn and I lived in northern Illinois at the time, far removed from the gigantic Independence Day revelry planned for the eastern population centers of New York City and our nation's capital. The harbors of Lake Michigan would not permit tall ships to gather and amaze shoreline watchers with their gallantry. We did not have a New York harbor where tons of fireworks had been assembled for a once-in-a-lifetime display.

Our community may have been outspent and out-glamorized, but we were not to be outdone. Tens of thousands gathered at the high school football stadium on that sultry Fourth of July evening for our own version of "once in a lifetime." There was a sense of community and shared pride that permeated the crowd. Idle chatter filled the air as we patiently waited for the daylight to fade. Bands stirred our passions with a medley of rousing marches and then urged our voices to blend together in the words of the familiar songs of patriotic fervor.

Freedom. What a precious gift we had inherited. It was a moment to celebrate and to share our love of country.

Darkness fell and sparklers glittered on the field to announce the launching of the long-anticipated pyrotechnic display. Bursting bombs filled the air with their acrid odor, and colorful cascading ribbons of brilliant light overwhelmed our senses. What a glorious feeling to be united—and free.

As I looked about me in a darkness illuminated by the rockets' red glare, I saw happy, smiling faces. But there was also an undercurrent of restlessness; this was but a respite from the tensions of tomorrow. These hours spent celebrating our common history would give way to the responsibilities of everyday life.

Then the question occurred to me. Are we really free? Our constitution guarantees freedom. We are not bound in the literal physical sense by real chains and shackles. In that sense we are free. But we *are* slaves in a literal spiritual sense. We are bound by our selfishness, by our pride. We are enslaved to our sin.

Our real freedom comes only because our Lord God sacrificed His Son to purchase it. With our redemption guaranteed through Christ, we are free to live in hope and joy. It is my prayer that this most precious gift of true freedom will always be yours.

Freedom

The sounding fury beat against our senses,
forcing from our lips a gasp,

While yet another messenger, carrying
aloft its festive tidings,

Etched a fiery pathway through the dark-
ened sky, there finally

To erupt in star-like glory, a cascade of
twinkling hues

So reminiscent of those inherent in this,
our nation's banner.

A swelling chorus, cloaked in awe,
burst forth from throat and lip.

Rising through the night air heavy with
an acrid haze and quivering echo,

It rendezvoused with flickering dying
remnants of what was recent splendor.

"Happy birthday, America!" A joyous
multitude, in gala mood,

Echoed and re-echoed that jubilant

refrain. "Happy birthday, America!"

Tear-streaked faces turned to one another in a newfound unity

As emotion-laden voices merged in anthem to this freedom-founded land.

Freedom, that precious concept, conceived in joy but born through agony

Nurtured in a multitude of breasts in days of triumph and hours of despair.

In times as long ago as Valley Forge and as new to us as Selma,

In places as far away as Iwo Jima and as near at hand as Gettysburg.

Freedom! The rapture of the moment enfolded us in womblike warmth

Unsurpassed by the summery July evening air that lay heavy upon us.

But were we really free, we who sang so lustily of that ideal?

Frozen in transitory bursts of stark illumination were those around me.

Features, carved by tools of tragedies in hands of time

Spoke vividly of habitual slavery and imprisonment by guilt.

Bound by envy, entwined in jealousy, shackled by fear,

Were we hopelessly ensnared in this, a web of our own making,

*Mere chattel whose true freedom must
remain forever an illusionary dream?*

*Listen, you who yearn to shed the shackles,
break the binding chains,*

*There is a key, a means whereby you can
be set at liberty!*

*Attune your ears, the message comes to
you at Christmastide,*

*Not garbed in tinsel or entwined in
ribbons bright,*

*But one of quiet stillness, humble birth,
and manger stall,*

*Of God's great love for you and me who
grapple with the foe.*

*Christ came to loose the captives, liberate
the slaves,*

*He is your Savior, come to truly set you
free.*

*He has sent me to bind up the brokenhearted, to pro-
claim freedom for the captives and release from darkness for
the prisoners.* Isaiah 61:1b

So if the Son sets you free, you will be free indeed.
John 8:36

GHOST WALK

The wood-burning stove, tucked into a bricked alcove on one side of our huge country kitchen, had spent the evening hours busily transforming hardwood chunks into glowing embers. Radiant waves of energy wormed their way into the bodies of those gathered around the table, enhancing the warmth of a family gathering. Separated from heaps of snow and teeth-chattering cold by a paned picture window, we felt safe, snug, and at peace. The sheltering confines of a home, designed to encompass the ecstatic antics of grandchildren, created a sense of sublime tranquility.

It was Christmas. The "oohs" and "aahs" of gift unwrapping had long since subsided. Into the resulting vacuum there flowed the final clatter of dishes being washed, dried, and stacked. Now, surrounded by children and grandchildren and in a setting that would have made Charles Dickens green with envy, we were all ready to settle down "for that long winter nap."

All, that is, except for two rambunctious 6-year-old grandchildren whose energy level still registered several notches above full. The accumulated excitement of the day refused to fade, even when "Don't you think it is bedtime?" was spoken. It soon became apparent that extreme measures would be required to still the two tempests, a task I reluctantly volunteered to undertake.

"Bradley and Morgan," I suggested, "would you like to go for a walk?" Their unified "Yes!" was immediately translated into a frantic search for appropriate clothing. Within minutes, three bundled-and-booted bodies were headed out the door.

The frigid night air nipped our nostrils and rouged our cheeks as we turned down the narrow snow-entrenched street leading to Lake Michigan. Pale rays from a distant streetlight created the necessary elements for a challenging "Shadow Stepping" game. Tiny feet dashed about in pursuit of a darting (surprisingly agile for his age) elusive target, with an occasional exultant shout "Grandpa, we stepped on you" signaling their success.

The sound of the tireless surf fell softly on our tingling ears as we abandoned the street to pursue an obscure path leading into the adjacent forest. Giant beech and maple trees formed a canopy of trellised twigs etched against the starlit sky. A gentle breeze moved through their midst, transforming them into the frightening arms and fingers of witches and goblins reaching out to grab us. A few vivid suggestions further sparked innocent imaginations. Within seconds, frightened squeals were bouncing off the snow that blanketed the foreboding forest.

Pint-sized mittened hands glued together in an attempt to multiply courage as they forged ahead of me. Engrossed in excited chatter and entranced by menacing shapes, they failed to notice that their trailing guide had silently vanished. The trunk of a huge beech tree and I, in dark clothing, had blended to become visibly one!

A precautionary backward glance from the diminutive twosome brought the startling realization that they seemed to be alone. A tremulous "Grandpa, are you there?" was heard. Their answer was a deafening silence! My low moan added to their anxiety but also directed their attention and hesitating steps in my direction. Hoping against hope that I was nearby, they whispered "Grandpa, we know that is you!" with all the bravado they could muster. The response was an ever-increasing eerie hush. Finally a tiny "meow" brought them close enough to see me.

As I knelt down they rushed into arms that quickly wrapped around them. Needless to say, three pairs of hands were inseparably linked for the remainder of the walk.

Frightening as it was at the time—and always would be in the future—a "Ghost Walk" became the number one request on all subsequent visits. And although it seems strange that they would want to repeat what they knew would be a frightening experience, I think I know why.

They trusted me. They had the calm assurance that their grandpa, who was intimately acquainted with every square inch of that dark forest floor, would always be nearby to protect them. They knew my arms would be waiting to welcome them with loving, reassuring hugs after it was over. They could cling to my hands and walk in the protection of my presence for the remainder of the evening.

Our future can very easily seem like a "Ghost Walk" as we contemplate what lies ahead. A year of tomorrows can appear dark and foreboding as we try to envision the shape of coming events. Just as goblin-like branches snagging a jacket in the darkness can evoke a child's frightened response, so the grasp of unanswerable questions evoke our anxiety. "Will I ever marry?" "Will our child resist temptation?" "Will we overcome the difficulties in our marriage?" "Will I be the victim of downsizing?" "Is that stabbing pain in my chest a heart attack?" "What will happen to my spouse should I die first?" "Will I be able to cope with the loneliness if I am the second to die?"

In panic we turn for help—only to find ourselves seemingly alone as we fail to see our God in the darkness of our fear. In desperation we call out a timid "God, where are You? I know You are there." The silence is broken by the whispered, "I am here as always, waiting for you in My Word."

As we run to that Word, we find precious promises that will never be broken. Encapsulated in familiar phrases are the sounds that give us direction and lead us to a loving Father. Listen to His voice as it comes to us:

"He who did not spare His own Son, but gave Him up for us all—how will He not also, along with Him, graciously give us all things? ... For I am convinced that neither death nor life, neither angels nor demons, neither the present nor the future, nor any powers, neither height nor depth, nor anything else in all creation, will be able to separate us from the love of God that is in Christ Jesus our Lord" (Romans 8:32, 38–39).

"Even though I walk through the valley of the shadow of death, I will fear no evil, for You are with me; Your rod and Your staff, they comfort me" (Psalm 23:4).

As we slowly edge closer in the direction of that voice, we see that He stands there, calling to us, always ready to enfold us in the warmth of His love.

Although coming days may bring moments of fear and anxiety, it is possible to follow the example of two grandchildren as we confidently walk down the path that leads into the forest of "tomorrow." For we are promised that our God, who is intimately familiar with every square millimeter of our shadowy future, will never leave us or forsake us. Although it seems to us that He momentarily vanishes from our sight, we know with absolute certainty that He is always there in the shadows, waiting with open arms. Then, as we continue our walk through the darkness, the warmth of His gentle grasp will give us the peace we desire.

That assurance is ours because of a series of events that began with the birth of the Christ Child in Bethlehem and led to a cross on Golgotha, culminating in a glorious resurrection. Redeemed child of God, may that confidence always reside within your breast.

For I am convinced that neither death nor life, neither angels nor demons, neither the present nor the future, nor any powers, neither height nor depth, nor anything else in all creation, will be able to separate us from the love of God that is in Christ Jesus our Lord. Romans 8:38–39

HAPPY NEW YEAR

That particular January 1 signaled the beginning of a year filled with indications that the world was collapsing around us. Not only did the nuclear threat continue to hang over our heads, but troubles from within were spawning feelings of gloom and despair.

The bitter aftertaste of the Vietnam War still lingered on our national taste buds. A divisive Watergate scandal continued to grow and flourish as one discovery led to another, with each an increasing threat to the most powerful position in our nation (and possibly the world). Lines were beginning to form at gas pumps while rumors concerning the pending energy crisis ran unchecked. Moral decay manifested itself in the form of crumbling marriages and changing sexual mores. Inflation was running rampant despite price controls that created shortages accompanied by dishonest practices.

It was a time when the storm clouds on the horizon

appeared so threatening that some married couples were questioning the wisdom of bringing a child into the world. Despite the apprehension, a birth in our family was welcomed with gratitude and pride. The reason was obvious to our family and friends. The new arrival was our first grandchild.

The memory of the inauguration of her first full year in our midst remains vivid. Only a grandparent can fully appreciate the emotions that result in tears of joy, hope, and nagging apprehension. It was uplifting and appealing to my manhood as I cuddled her, my arms forming a protective shield. It was quite the opposite to contemplate my impotence in shaping the future. Would her adult world, a distant dream at that moment, be one of unlimited opportunity? Or would it be one of unbounded despair?

A glance out our kitchen window didn't help. The savagery of winter had long since stripped the vegetation of summer garb while heaping mounds of snow in its stead. Contemplating the glacial winds whipping off the lake further enhanced my gloomy outlook for the future. At the moment I felt helpless and hopeless.

My dismal thoughts were interrupted by the flight of sparrows crossing my plane of vision, their destination a well-stocked feeder nearby. I watched as a dozen balls of fluffed feathers scrambled for position amidst the scattered grains. Conspicuous by its absence was any indication of depressed spirits or display of worried postures. Instead I witnessed an unbridled exuberance for life.

How different from the attitude I was displaying. Why should I feel helpless when the world outside the window was a showcase for God's creative power and divine providence? How could I, who had celebrated the birth of Christ just one week ago, so quickly forget the love God demonstrated when He lived among His people? What egotism and self-centeredness to even imagine that the future of this precious infant depended on my abilities and authority. She was God's own.

Peace returned as I placed her slumbering body in her Father's waiting arms.

"Happy New Year, my little one,
Your first to celebrate upon this earth."
Deep desires were gently whispered
To a daughter's daughter, cuddled close,
Cherubic brow warming the hollow of my cheek.
Delicate fragrance, enveloping my nostrils,
Saturated my being with sheer delight.

Happy New Year? The reverie was shattered!
In its stead the icy grasp of deep dismay
Unrelentingly clutched my inner self.
Corruption? Moral Decay? Strife?
Recession? Inflation? Energy Crisis?

Were all opportunities for happiness to be denied
This tiny being so dear to me?

Dark foreboding clouds filled my mind,
Obscuring the light of hope, and joy, and peace.
I held her close as sympathy engulfed me,
And anguish surged within my throbbing heart,
Aching, in marked contrast to her calm repose.

My loved one stirred, and seeming to sense
The strife within me, lifted her head.
The serenity of her gaze engaged my troubled eye.
"Grandpa," her glance conveyed, "have you so soon
Forgotten Him of whom just yesterday you sang?
Did you leave Christ in Christmas?"

Had I forgotten?
Forgotten Him, who once had pledged
That He would never leave me or forsake me?
Forgotten Him, when sounding surf reminded me
That even wind and waves obeyed His voice?

Forgotten Him? A saucy sparrow gaily chirped
Beyond the sheltering glass, its spirit undimmed
By winter's frigid blast. "My Father provides,"
His carefree manner said. "His love for you
Is so much more. Why is your faith so small?"

Forgotten Him? In shame I saw
The lack of faith and trust in Him, my Lord.
"Forgive me, God," I cried. "Restore to me
The faith of this, your little one."

My prayer was heard, for quickly as they came
The clouds dispersed, and in their stead
The warmth of hope and joy encompassed me.
My lips caressed her cheek as peace returned,
And once again our hearts beat as one.

You will keep in perfect peace him whose mind is stead-
fast, because he trusts in You. Trust in the LORD forever, for
the LORD, the LORD, is the Rock eternal. Isaiah 26:3–4

LITTLE PEOPLE

Some things are too painful to recall much less share. It can result from either a wrong done to us or by us. In either case, a lingering feeling of anger, guilt, or shame often makes us reluctant to expose the event to the light of day. Such has been my situation in regard to an incident that took place on our wedding day.

It was quite natural that Lynn and I should meet via a blind date. After all she was an air evac nurse newly-arrived at Clark Field in the Philippine Islands, and I was a troop carrier pilot who frequently flew air evac missions. It didn't take me long to realize that this was the young lady with whom I wanted to spend the rest of my days. Her acceptance of my proposal in mid-July was followed by an immediate decision to set August 15 as our wedding date. We couldn't have known that VJ day, which had seemed so unattainable a month before, would fall on our chosen day. Nor could we foresee the last minute confusion this historic moment would add to an event already laced with frantic preparation.

It is impossible to imagine the innovation required to plan a wedding when both parties were flying combat missions while living in a land torn apart by the ravages of war. A white parachute, treasured souvenir of the paratroop drop on Corregidor, was transformed into a negligee and pajamas by the imagination and skilled fingers of a local seamstress. Somehow we located a chaplain. Although hospitalized with hepatitis, he obtained a pass for the afternoon and performed the ceremony in the thatch-roofed chapel of the 46th Troop Carrier Squadron. The prominent Manila family we had helped rescue from prison five months earlier arranged the rental of several rooms in one of the few remaining homes. Our commanding general surprised us by loaning his car and driver for our honeymoon journey, and the Navy furnished the wedding cake and a professional photographer.

I can still see Lynn coming down the packed-dirt aisle on the arm of her squadron adjutant. Prior military training ensured that each step precisely followed the rhythm determined by the organist valiantly pumping the pedals of the field organ. At his side stood a violinist whose civilian job was with the Boston Symphony. The ceremony that followed is a blur in my memory, although the vows we exchanged have never been forgotten.

The photographer faithfully recorded everything that took place on that humid tropical afternoon. He captured Lynn's beautiful smile as she came down the aisle. He recorded the faces of the many friends from both squadrons offering their congratulations. He accompanied us to the day room of the nurse's quarters and recorded on film the traditional activities of a wedding reception.

On the evening of the seventh day of our honeymoon, an ambulance (no jeeps were available) from Lynn's squadron appeared at the doorstep of our "villa." The driver informed us that he had orders to transport us back to Clark Field without delay. Lynn's unit was being transferred to Okinawa and was scheduled to fly out within a matter of hours.

The next morning we shared a tearful good-bye as my bride climbed aboard the waiting C-47. Soon I was experiencing the piercing pangs of a newly discovered loneliness as I watched the plane disappear into the pre-dawn darkness. Our parting agreement was for me to track down the photographer and get copies (and hopefully the negatives) of the pictures he had taken.

It was mid-morning before I was able to locate the Navy unit of the elusive shutterbug. I have a vivid memory of entering the Quonset hut and seeing the young enlisted man sitting on the edge of his cot. My friendly greeting brought a heads-down grunt in response. His reply to my eager request to view the wedding pictures was a gruff, "They are not available. You will have to see my commanding officer."

Sensing a problem, I hurried to the office of the CO. After I identified myself and stated my request, he said, "Please sit down, I want to talk to you." Responding to my puzzled look, he continued, "Let me explain the reason for his refusal. That young photographer voluntarily devoted an entire afternoon and evening to this assignment, spending hours of his time to record scene after scene. Yet during all that activity he was never once recognized or thanked. No one asked him to join the reception festivities. He was never offered a drink, invited to partake of the buffet and cake, or dance with one of the nurses. He was treated as though he didn't exist, and this hurt him so deeply that I agree with his refusal to give you the pictures."

I went back to the young man with a heavy heart and new understanding. The next quarter-hour was spent in explaining, apologizing, pleading, offering monetary rewards, and even shedding a few tears of remorse. It was to no avail. The photographs of our wedding were gone forever.

For years I nursed a mixture of shame and anger when recalling that August afternoon. My understanding of our mistreatment of him did nothing to extinguish a smoldering anger. It flared up every time I thought of having been denied possession of the visual reminders of the beginning of our life together. But with the passage of time, God has healed that painful wound and transformed it into a twofold enriching experience.

First, He has helped me acquire eyes that recognize and lips ready to thank those often treated as "little people." They are the ones we "look through" as they perform a menial task, the waitress at a table, a maid in a hotel, a custodian at a church, or even that wife or husband or child who is taken for granted. Sincerely thanking someone and then seeing their joyful response reflected in their eyes has done the job. With the passage of time, the anger I harbored was gradually neutralized.

Second, I now realize that "little people" play a very important role in God's plan of redemption for His children. The long anticipated birth of the Savior was announced first to the lowly shepherds, who many considered to be the scum of society. Jesus shunned the inhabitants of royal palaces so He could visit the lonely and downtrodden and eat with those despised by the ruling gentry. He rebuked His followers for their condescending attitude toward the children He gathered in His arms. His disciples were fishermen chosen for their willingness to follow rather than for prestigious positions or prominence in the community.

There have also been times during the years since our wedding when I found myself in the role of "little people." I can attest to the pain of going unrecognized that results when others "look through" you. I have been disheartened by the realization that I am a tiny minnow in a pond of trophy fish.

Fortunately the negative feelings have become increasingly fleeting. Rather than relying on human opinion to bolster my ego, I have learned to turn to the only reliable source for self-evaluation—God's Word. There I find that who I am and what I have accomplished on my own is not acknowledged by my Father. Whether I am the president of our nation or a custodian in charge of restrooms is of little consequence in His sight.

It is not my personal stature that makes me visible in the Lord's eyes. It is instead the cloak of Christ's righteousness, which He has placed on my shoulders, that makes me stand out in the crowd. His unconditional love "sees" me even when as I remain unrecognized by the world. He forgives my faults and enables me to forgive others. His hand reaches out and accepts me as I am. As a result, no matter how "little" I may feel when compared to others, I know I will always be number one in God's eyes.

Before I formed you in the womb I knew you, before you were born I set you apart. Jeremiah 1:5a

Therefore, whoever humbles himself like this child is the greatest in the kingdom of heaven. Matthew 18:4

LOST

I have many vivid memories of the winter I spent at Coffeyville Army Air Field in Kansas. I can still see the tarpapered barracks and feel the chill of the winter wind that penetrated the walls. I can still hear the juke box in the cramped snack bar as it played songs that added to the misery of my first-ever Christmas away from home. I can still feel the resilient boardwalks that enabled us to cross the sea of mud separating the barracks from the road. And I can still smell the cockpit odors of the trusty BT13 Vultee Vibrator in which we were trained.

Sharpest of all my memories, however, is that of my first cross-country flight that January. Among our many assignments were several weeks of navigation classes in preparation for an initial jaunt beyond the friendly environs of home base. That journey was supposed to take us from Coffeyville to Pittsburg, Kansas, about 60 miles to the northeast. There we were required to land and check in with our instructor before proceeding another 60 miles due west to Independence, Kansas, where a new training field was under construction. Another landing and check-in, and we were off on the 20-mile southerly flight to our home base.

The course was carefully plotted on a sectional map. Each would-be pilot spent hours preparing a card on which he listed every conceivable checkpoint found on the map. Our accumulated distance and flying time calculations were painstakingly recorded. Our weatherman confidently predicted a strong wind from the south. This information was penciled into our reliable plotters from which we then calculated the precise "crab angle" needed to remain on course.

Our takeoffs were staggered to prevent any attempts at a follow-the-leader routine. I waited nervously for several minutes before I found myself noisily intruding in "the untrespassed sanctity of space." Altitude, compass heading, airspeed, time—my eyes kept moving back and forth to prevent undue concentration on one or the other.

"Time is up," I told myself. "That first checkpoint should be showing up." A country road and a small bridge across a stream were supposed to be visible below my right wingtip. One big problem—I could not detect the slightest resemblance between marks on the map and the landscape below. Tinges of panic began replacing what had been an anxious complacency.

"Hold your heading, fly the required time, and you'll be okay." I kept repeating the phrase with a smattering of false bravado. That was shattered when the moment known as "Expected Time of Arrival" appeared on my clock—with no airstrip in sight. At that point one thought became dominant. The south wind had been stronger than predicted, and I had drifted north of my course. It never dawned on me that the meteorologist could have been wrong.

A circle to the right revealed a town nestled in the barren countryside. "Read the name from the sign on the outskirts, and then you will know where you are." A superb low-level approach brought me to an altitude of 50 feet above the road. At that point I could decipher the name on the sign. "Weir," it stated. I regained altitude and redirected my attention to the map and the area north of my destination. Unfortunately, the northern border of the sectional map ended just above Pittsburg. The name "Weir" was nowhere to be seen.

I panicked as all attempts at rational thinking were reduced to hopelessness. I had flown beyond the boundaries of the map! It would be impossible to find the airfield since I didn't know where to look! I continued my desperate circling while searching for a solution. I finally saw a farmer on a level field below. By then I was so frightened that I did what my wife Lynn claims could never happen—I decided to ask for directions.

"Dragging the field" with wheels several feet off the ground revealed an acceptably level grassy surface. A standard right hand approach led to one of my better landings. I raised the flaps, cranked open the canopy, and taxied to where a puzzled farmer was waiting. As I approached, I shouted, "Where is Pittsburg?" His hand pointed—north! *North! It can't be,"* I said to myself. A quick glance at the map revealed he was right. There, south of the course line I had drawn, was a dot with "Weir" beside it. My hurried and embarrassed "Thanks" was followed by a takeoff that barely cleared the trees because I had forgotten to properly position the flaps. I now pointed the nose north, and in a few minutes the runway was dead ahead.

A frantic instructor (who told me later he had given me up for lost) was so relieved that he forgot to ask for an explanation. His radioed instruction, which I gratefully obeyed, was to immediately take off for Independence. Again I followed the prepared flight plan, following precisely the pre-calculated heading I had noted on my card. All the while I silently repeated the navigation classroom mantra, "weathermen are always right." Again I covered mile after mile without recognizing a single checkpoint.

In time, however, a huge sigh of relief erupted when, at the proper moment, an airfield loomed dead ahead. Imagine my embarrassment when a closer look revealed the familiar contours of, not Independence, but Coffeyville. A north wind, coupled with my stubborn determination to correct for an opposite breeze, brought me 20 miles south of the specified goal. In exasperation, I called the control ship at Independence and told them that I would be landing at Coffeyville and calling it a day.

Half-hour later a livid lieutenant met me in front of base operations. His scathing comments regarding my flying ability remained sequestered, as did my "emergency" landing, until after I received my silver wings the following April.

One of the consequences of my first attempts at flight navigation was that my instructor occupied the back seat on my next cross country. I never got lost again, even during the years I negotiated the uncharted jungles of New Guinea. But I still doubt weather forecasts.

The memory of the panic I felt that day can still twist my stomach. It happened on another occasion while I was on a solitary hike deep within snow-covered mountains. I had used a rocky promontory to guide my footsteps during an hour-long journey, and now it was time to return. In the meantime, low-hanging clouds had stolen my navigation crutch, the sun. After walking for a half-hour I came upon footprints—my own. The straight line I thought was leading me to my car had somehow become a circle. It took all the discipline I could muster to suppress a mind-paralyzing panic.

Have you had a similar experience? It can happen on a dark night when all sense of direction vanishes. A sightseeing expedition that ends up in an unfamiliar neighborhood can trigger a similar response. If comparable occurrences have been yours, then the momentary taste of terror may still linger in your memory.

Getting lost can also happen as we navigate our way through life. We can lose someone close to us and unexpectedly find ourselves circling in the unknown mists of loneliness. The clouds that gather as we hear a dreaded diagnosis from our doctor can hide our guiding light. Years can be spent carefully charting a course for our self and our family with all checkpoints carefully noted. Suddenly an unforeseen event such as family breakup, loss of job, or financial setback makes the landscape unrecognizable.

We begin to circle, looking for something that might help us find our way out of our lost condition and ease the panic that has us in its grip. We fly low enough to recognize names of towns such as "psychiatry," "counseling," "drugs," or "alcohol," only to find that they cannot be found on the map we have been using. In a frantic effort we decide to ask for directions. The field we select for our emergency landing is Word and Sacrament. We shout out our request and God points us in the right direction—back toward His Son, our Lord and Savior, Jesus Christ.

But He doesn't let us fly solo. The Holy Spirit climbs in the backseat and teaches us how to find our way through a wilderness of unmarked territory using charts and maps found only in Holy Scripture. The compass of His love leads us to the forgiveness that is ours through His means of grace. And after a lifetime of flying, He will be there to guide us to the Eternal Landing Strip where we will hangar our aircraft forever. All travels thereafter will be made in the light of God's glory.

"Be strong and courageous. Do not be terrified; do not be discouraged, for the LORD your God will be with you wherever you go." Joshua 1:9

THROUGH THE
PORTHOLE

This was not what we had anticipated!

Our flight to Fairbanks in mid-July had enabled us to finally say "We have set foot in all 50 states!" Several days later, an afternoon train ride took us through a mountain and to the dock where the cruise ship waited. Our Alaskan cruise that had nestled in our dreams for years was about to begin.

We were quickly absorbed in a mass of disgorged rail passengers surging up the gangplank to the ship. There the throng fragmented as individuals ran up and down hallways in search of assigned quarters. We located ours after descending a number of decks below the luxury level. Although deep in the bowels of the ship, it had a porthole that permitted a limited view of the outside world.

The first two days featured nonstop eating, placid waters, brilliant sunshine, and breathtaking views.

Excess calories were consumed (or so we told ourselves) in numerous forays up and down the stairs. There was also an endless dashing from one side of the ship to the other, camera in hand, in pursuit of the perfect view that would incite the envy of friends and, we hoped, enrich Kodak's coffers.

We were awakened on that third morning by an ominous change in pulsing rhythm of the engines. Suspended items, stationary the night before, were swaying wildly from their moorings. Most frightening of all was the view from the porthole. The placid ocean surface of the previous days had disappeared. Instead, we saw glass submerged in the foaming spray and green waters of a raging sea. For an instant we were overcome by the sickening feeling that our *Princess* was on her way to becoming another *Titanic*.

After hurriedly throwing on clothes and tossing down Dramamine, we made our way to that place of solace and refuge, the dining room. It was an up-and-down journey fraught with peril as we clung to railings to maintain stability. The waiters were not so fortunate. Panic clouded their features as they sought to maintain their footing while balancing trays loaded with breakfast vittles.

A warming tray flew off a stand, scattering burning Sterno cans across the floor. Dishes slid over the tablecloths stained with spills. A woman tipped over backward in her chair. Electrifying the atmosphere was the pervasive feeling that all was not well. We were in the midst of a ferocious Alaskan gulf storm, and the view outside indicated our troubles were serious.

Seeking reassurance, I made my way to the wheelhouse. Expecting to find a sense of urgency, I saw instead that the captain was seated on a stool calmly directing the activities of his crew. With radar piercing the veil of the storm and satellites beaming a space view of cloud formations, he had all the information necessary for safe navigation. He knew his ship, he knew where we were, and he knew his storms. Desperate as it appeared to me, to him it was just another day of keeping the bow pointed into the waves while maintaining course for the haven his charts told him was straight ahead.

We spend our days sailing across adventurous seas aboard the cruise ship "Life's Journey." Although we would love a stateroom with a picture window on the veranda deck, our assigned quarters are equipped instead with just a tiny porthole. Rather than having a panoramic view of tomorrow, we are permitted to see only the single moment at hand.

Most days are spent gazing out that small circular window at glassy seas and sunny skies. However, times come when apprehension awakens us and we look through a porthole submerged in the surging seas of adversity. Unexpected illness, family difficulties, faith struggles, the death of a loved one, unemployment, debilitating demands on our time—each is a storm that can strike terror in our heart.

Fearing for our very existence and trying anxiously to catch a glimpse of the future, we turn to family and friends for support and assurance. To our dismay, we find that their view is identical to ours. Their view is obliterated by the frothy sea. All they can feel is a thrashing ship. All they can offer is the solace of being fellow travelers.

In desperation we make our painful way to the wheelhouse called "God's Word." There we see the Captain, our Heavenly Father, calmly guiding our ship through the turbulent waters of life. His eyes pierce the fog to detect obstacles. His voice reassures us that we are safe. He knows our exact position.

We know our ship will not flounder because He has promised that His hand will never leave the wheel. Standing at His side are His two chief officers, our Lord Jesus Christ and the Holy Spirit. Together they take us through the storm while maintaining course for the haven that lies ahead. Although shrouded in fog, we know that a heavenly harbor is ahead. That is why our view through the porthole need never cause fear.

So we fix our eyes not on what is seen, but on what is unseen. For what is seen is temporary, but what is unseen is eternal. 2 Corinthians 4:18

LITTLEST SNOWFLAKE

The variety of plants encountered on a summertime walk through the countryside is almost overwhelming. Some reach toward the heavens, others hug the breast of Mother Earth. Leaves and blossoms assume every shape and color imaginable.

I am always amazed by the infinite care and ingenuity exhibited by our Creator to ensure that each plant was designed for a distinct function. Most apparent is the way in which plants are used to carry out the overall plan of nature. As an example, some grow in the harsh environment of a sand dune along the lakeshore, providing stabilization to the shifting soil. Others are at home in the dank swamp where the decaying vegetation is slowly transformed into a soil in which other plants can then grow. Some provide nectar and in the process are pollinated by one form of insect, while a neighbor may attract a totally different clientele.

Each has a place, each has a purpose, all work together in harmony to carry out God's great design.

How different it is with people. We tend to give honor to the mighty few and look upon the millions of "little people" as being unimportant. The unfortunate part is that we often experience the sting of being looked upon as useless and begin to believe that we are of little value, even within God's Church. As a result we develop low self-esteem, a feeling of having been "behind the door" when the Holy Spirit was passing out gifts.

This feeling amplifies as we grow older and leave behind the things that at one time made us feel useful. "Nobody needs me," we say to ourselves. "If only God would have given me some other gift, the ability that so-and-so has, then I could do something great for Him and be needed."

In Romans 12 the Lord tells us that people are similar to plants in that He has made both in a seemingly endless variety of forms and differing abilities. Moreover, He did it with a definite purpose in mind. Just like the plants, we are handcrafted to be a part of God's grand design. Each of us forms a part of the body of Christ, each of us has a function to carry out in God's great design for His Church.

Many of us may feel insignificant when we compare ourselves to others. We struggle to find a sense of self-worth, particularly during difficult times of our lives. But that is only because we fail to see ourselves through the eyes of our Father.

Following is a story about the Littlest Snowflake that I hope will help you understand the "reflecting role" for which God has prepared us.

A forlorn figure huddled within a secluded corner of Great White Cloud that drifted slowly over the wintry landscape far below. The bitter pain of rejection Littlest Snowflake was feeling was evident by the channel of tears that trickled downward.

"Why must I be so tiny and insignificant, so plain?" he thought. "Who would ever want to use me, especially when nobody seems to know that I exist? Why, oh why, did Mighty Father make me this way?"

Just then a flock of Feathery Flakes floated by. Littlest Snowflake was ashamed of his size and appearance, and so he tried to hide deeper within the folds of Great White Cloud. All his efforts were in vain, for he could not evade their disdainful glance. "Look at you," they chortled, "so frail and drab! Mighty Father made us big, soft, and fluffy so he might blanket the earth with our beauty. But you, so tiny and dull. ..." Mercifully their remaining remarks faded away in the distance, leaving behind a tiny snowflake who would have given anything if he could have just melted away.

A few hours later the Slithery Sleet squadron came into view. Their steely glance pierced the wispy cover that Littlest Snowflake was pulling over himself. "What a weakling," they hissed as they darted past. "Our stinging power can cause the bravest of men to cringe, and our strength can bend the mightiest tree. But what can you do?" Leaving behind words dripping with scorn, they dashed from Great White Cloud and flung themselves at the occupants of the land below.

Day after day Great White Cloud drifted along with the agony of loneliness piercing deeper and deeper into the heart of Littlest Snowflake. He watched as Mighty Father sent flocks of Feathery Flakes on their missions, guiding them as they floated gently down to the waiting arms of tree and shrub. He tried to vicariously share the tingle of excitement others felt as they discussed the thrilling adventures that lay before them. Everyone was busy, everybody had a purpose, each felt they were a part of the Father's plan. Everyone that is, except Littlest Snowflake. It seemed like Mighty Father did not even know that he existed. "I feel so worthless," he thought hopelessly. "Why, oh why, was I ever made?"

It was late in the evening of the following day when Mighty Father came into Great White Cloud. Everyone was surprised because he never came at this time of the day. They crowded around him, expecting the announcement of some new and exciting mission. Mighty Father glanced over the assembled group, but couldn't seem to find the one he was looking for. He moved the hovering flocks of Feathery Flakes to one side and sent the Slithery Sleet squadrons to a far corner. Then, reaching into a secluded nook, he gently gathered into his hand a trembling Littlest Snowflake.

"Littlest Snowflake," he said, "tonight I am asking you to perform a very special task for me."

"But Mighty Father," he replied, "haven't you made a mistake? Are you sure you want me? Look at me, I am so tiny, and plain, and weak. Don't you want someone else?"

"No, Littlest Snowflake," Mighty Father responded, "I want you! I made you just as you are so I could use you for this special purpose. I want you to come with me now, for it is time to leave!"

"Where am I going, and how shall I find my way? It is so dark outside!" Question after question tumbled from Littlest Snowflake as his excitement grew.

"Don't worry," replied Mighty Father, "I have provided a guidance system so you will not get lost. See," he pointed to the land beneath them, "there is a beam of light extending from that distant star to the earth below. I will place you on it. Follow this beam and it will lead you to your destination."

Littlest Snowflake grasped the shaft of light as Mighty Father gently released him from his hand. Slowly he started to slide away from the familiar environs of Great White Cloud and found himself entering the enveloping shroud of darkness beneath. His speed began to build rapidly as descended.

The inky blackness smothered his senses and anxieties crowded in upon him as he remembered his frailties. Would he be able to hold on? Was the task that he had been given too big for him? Feelings of apprehension flooded his mind, crowding out the memory of Mighty Father's gentle hand and loving concern.

Suddenly the darkness was shattered by a burst of light, and Littlest Snowflake found himself surrounded by a group of beings of indescribable brilliance and beauty. Songs of praise and adoration were pouring from their lips, and the harmony of voices was complemented by visages reflecting peace and tranquility. One of them broke away from the group and came to Littlest Snowflake.

"Don't be frightened," she said. "We are the Angelic Host, and I am Tiniest Angel. I will accompany you for the rest of the journey. See, there is our destination."

Peering through the darkness, Littlest Snowflake could barely discern the outline of a crude shed built of stones and poles. One side, sheltered from the wind, was open, and from it there emanated an ethereal glow.

As they drew nearer, the forms of people could be seen within the structure. Animals were bedded down nearby. In the center rested a crib meant to hold feed for the animals. Tonight, however, it contained something more precious! There, wrapped in layers of cloth, lay a tiny newborn baby. Mysteriously, that crib was the source of the glow that permeated the darkness.

A hush fell over the Angelic Host, and a look of reverence and awe dominated their features as they hovered overhead. Then the soft strains of a joyous hymn floated through the stillness of the night air. "Fear not," they sang, and the words echoed throughout the surrounding hills.

"Who is this?" whispered Littlest Snowflake, overcome by the wonder of the moment.

"This is Mighty Father's Only Son," said Tiniest Angel. "Come with me. Mighty Father made you, carefully formed you just as you are, so you might be the first jewel in Only Son's crown. Come, let me place you there."

Tiniest Angel gently positioned Littlest Snowflake on a curly lock of hair that rested in the center of Only Son's forehead. As Littlest Snowflake came in contact with that tiny head, a wonderful thing happened. Suddenly his frailty, the source of so much anguish, vanished. In its place came the strength that he had always longed for. Anxiety and despair, so long his companions, vanished. In their place peace, joy, and a sense of purpose.

The rays of the warm glow radiating from the innocent features of Only Son struck the many facets of Littlest Snowflake and, reflecting in all directions, transformed him into a sparkling gem of dazzling splendor admired by all.

Yet deep inside he recognized that he was still Littlest Snowflake, and that his newfound worth and beauty was only a reflection of the love, strength, and glory of Only Son!

⁓

"Just as each of us has one body with many members, and these members do not all have the same function, so in Christ we who are many form one body, and each member belongs to all the others. We have different gifts, according to the grace given us. ..." Romans 12:4–6a

BUT ALWAYS DAY BY DAY

Birds have been a part of my life for as long as I can remember. It was a love-hate relationship during my boyhood days on a Wisconsin farm, with the lowly English sparrows and their messy nesting habits the primary focus of my youthful wrath. A letter from my mother changed my perspective. Written during their retirement years, it described the joy she and Dad shared as they sat at the kitchen table and watched birds congregate at the feeder outside the window. Her vivid portrayal awakened within me a desire to do likewise.

Our home in Michigan gave me a place where I could finally satisfy that yearning. Our huge yard, abounding in trees that blended into the bordering ancient beech forest, was the ideal habitat for a wide variety of feathered friends. It also provided the opportunity to place a bird feeder outside the kitchen window. The design of the feeder was my original—a large open platform with lots of room for birds to assemble. Shielding the food from the elements was a roof supported by boards with heart-shaped cutouts.

A mid-September trip to the local feed store became an annual ritual. Shock absorbers groaned in response to the weight of an assortment of 50-pound bags of seed packed into every nook and cranny in our spacious family sedan. A short trip home and the process was reversed, with the food supply now carefully stacked in a sheltered corner near the feeder.

The arrival of winter signaled the start of a pre-dawn routine. Donning a down jacket, gloves, and boots as shields against the frigid winds off Lake Michigan, I would carefully brush new-fallen snow from the feeding platform and surrounding area. Scoops of seeds from bags in the storehouse replenished an avian smorgasbord diminished in quantity and quality by the diners of the previous day. Filling the heated water dish to the brim completed my labor of love.

As I entered the kitchen, radiant energy from a blazing wood-burning stove enveloped my body and quickly dispersed the accumulated chill. A steaming cup of coffee accompanied me to the chair and table adjoining the picture window as I awaited the arrival of dawn. Soon Lynn would join me to share the joy of watching dozens upon dozens of birds arriving to acquire the sustenance necessary to survive the harsh reality of winter for another day.

The variety of birds visiting our feeder seemed endless. Blue jays, cardinals, evening and morning grosbeaks, nuthatches, goldfinches, purple finches, shrikes, downy woodpeckers, sparrows—all made their rounds while adding their bit of color. Each exhibited a characteristic personality and feeding habit. At the bottom of the list was the occasional hawk that insisted on being part of the experience.

It was the chickadees, however, that captured my heart with their feisty spirit and sprightly air. They were the first to arrive in the morning and the last to leave at night. Exhibiting a trust beyond my comprehension, they would gather at the sound of my plaintive "chick-a-dee-dee-dee" and fearlessly fly to my outstretched palm to take the proffered sunflower seeds in their tiny beak.

Watching them day after day was a lesson in trust and faith that is still with me. My confidence in tomorrow is renewed as I compare my frail human efforts to faithfully provide daily provisions for some of God's creatures with my Heavenly Father's unbreakable promises to do the same for me. For His grace and mercy surpass any human effort; each day I am renewed in His love and forgiveness, enabled to live each day to the fullest.

(What I imagine the chickadee might
think and say)

I saw you there, bundled as you were
against the wintry blast,

A shadowy figure in the cast-iron gray of
fast approaching morn

That battled rigid ranks of snowy crystals
which in hours past

Had buried deep our sustenance you
yesterday had borne.

I watched, from perch secure within my
sheltering piney bed,

As ermine blanket soon made way for
lavish spread of favored seed

And knew, that for the hours of the day
that lay ahead,

A banquet table there was laid to meet
our every need.

I saw you there, enthralled as messengers
from newly wakened sun

Called forth a horde of feathery friends
from far and wide

Who, breaking now a fast that seemed to
them so long ago begun,

Consumed in haste the bounty you so
graciously supplied.

I watched as, smile upon your lips, you
turned to opened door

*Where deep within the ripened fruits of
harvest in abundance lay*

*And there, with Magi-wisdom born of
that which went before,*

*Brought forth more sustenance, enough to
last for just that day.*

*I saw you there, head bared to warming
rays of heaven's greater light,*

*As I came near on wings with laughter
filled and joy I could not hide.*

*Expecting mirrored peace, your face
reflected more the shade of night*

*As furrows etched upon your brow told
tales of struggles deep inside.*

*I watched—your troubled eyes bespoke of
mind in haste to chart a course*

*Down dark and secret-shrouded paths
that in the far-off future lay,*

*The same ingenious mind that had in
days past built a bounteous source*

*And wisely now directs that all our needs
be met, but always day-by-day.*

*(My response to the chickadee's imagined
observations)*

*I saw you there, in impish flight that
brought you to my beckoning hand,*

*Your minute black-capped body vibrant
with the sheer exuberance of life,*

And there you paused upon my palm, in
trust that all I would command

Was only for your good—to shield you
from all evil, harm, and strife.

I watched—and then myself I saw within
the concave of God's hand of love,

And peace came o'er me as, while
nestling there, I heard my Father say,

"Whatever happens falls within My
power, and as I watch you from above

From My abundant grace I'll meet your
needs—but always day by day!"

"Look at the birds of the air; they do not sow or reap or
store away in barns, and yet your heavenly Father feeds them.
Are you not much more valuable than they?" Matthew 6:26

How much more did God's grace and the gift that came
by the grace of the one man, Jesus Christ, overflow to the
many! Romans 5:15b

THE COVER-UP

Have you ever thought about the planning and foresight displayed by the almighty Lord in His creation? I sometimes make an effort to visualize the perfect world that He made. I try to envision a Garden of Eden where everyone and everything existed in perfect harmony. We learn in Genesis 1:29–30 that all creatures ate plants and seeds for food. Everyone was an herbivore. How different from the world that exists today.

Why the dramatic difference? The drama recorded in Genesis 3 offers the explanation. It was Adam and Eve's desire to know evil that changed all of creation. Their human nature changed from the selflessness God created them with to a new natural selfishness. Their fall to temptation also affected every aspect of a creation that God had earlier declared to be very good. Sin had entered the world. The first death of animals recorded in Genesis 3:21 was an immediate consequence. Thorns and thistles grew as the ground was cursed. Pain and suffering became a part of life. The food chain as we now know it sprang into being.

Consequently a delicate balance of nature exists today, one in which predator and disease are used to keep plant, animal, and insect populations in control. I found a perfect example the year we moved to our northern Michigan home. The cottontail rabbit population had recently undergone a tenfold multiplication, and we were in danger of becoming an embattled minority. Coinciding with this situation was a similar increase in the number of skunks. The resulting predator/prey relationship stabilized the overall community, and that is why that year became known as the year of the skunks.

It was also our first year as managers of RKD, a family camp situated on a beautiful Lake Michigan white-sand beach. Mid-June had arrived and with it an onslaught of 150 energetic teenagers eager to begin their week-long retreat experience. The 45 rooms of the two-story inn were packed with bodies and excitement. Our task was to ensure that the walls remained intact and the roof stayed in place.

Assisting me in my duties was Beau Jo, our beautiful five-year-old blond cocker spaniel. It was late in the evening of our second day and every effort was being made to secure the lid we were trying to clamp on the day's activities. The final hallway patrol had been completed and I was entertaining the thought of a stroll on the beach where balmy lake breezes could sooth nerves frayed by tension.

A moment later my embryonic dream of peace was shattered by a crescendo of piercing screams emanating from the inn. Panic surged through my body with the dreaded thought of fire uppermost in my mind. But the reason for the bedlam became apparent midway in my mad dash for the door. The acrid pungent odor of skunk musk assaulted my senses as it began to penetrate my nostrils and overwhelm my olfactory nerves. Seeping through screened windows, it was filling rooms with a suffocating odor while simultaneously emptying them of occupants. Calm was restored after assuring the chattering teens that death was not imminent.

I retraced my steps to find the instigator of the upheaval. It was a mission quickly accomplished. Apparently Beau Jo's adventurous prowling of the bushes bordering the inn had been enlivened by an encounter with a skunk. It was the former who had challenged and the latter who had won what probably began as a test of masculinity. By the time I arrived, a thoroughly vanquished canine was frantically rolling in the sand in a vain attempt to expunge the fiery "skunk's revenge" from his senses.

Burying his head in the icy waters of the lake may

have cooled eyes and nose, but it did nothing for the malodorous condition of his body. Nor could he understand why our relationship had changed dramatically. Hands that had earlier stroked his body were now extended in an effort to keep him at a comfortable distance. A voice formerly laced with love now carried overtones of rebuke.

This was but the prelude to the ultimate rebuff. The one who loved to sleep cuddled against my legs at the foot of the bed was surprised to learn that he would spend the night locked in the entry room to our small cottage. Never did body language so vividly portray the pain of rejection.

The next morning Beau Jo's wagging tail and pleading eyes gave clear evidence of his desire to make amends. It was all to no avail. My companion remained sequestered in the cottage while I pursued office duties and searched for ways to deodorize him.

The program director's entreaty, "Would you take a group of kids on a hike up the beach," interrupted my duties. The beckoning sun glistening off sparkling blue waves and white sand ensured that "Yes" was the immediate answer. Within minutes I was heading south with a half dozen teenagers in tow.

As we passed our cottage it was mutually agreed that Beau Jo could accompany us. His joy was clearly evident, although by now he seemed to realize that his condition had somehow changed our relationship. He appeared to understand the desirability of exploring the beach at some distance from our group.

We were amused by his investigative antics and then surprised when he stopped to roll in the sand. It was evident that he was enjoying the sensation because he twisted and turned his body to ensure that every square inch was covered. As we approached, he stopped, rose to his feet, and then ran toward us. His wagging tail and happy expression indicated that something positive had taken place.

As he came near we realized what it was. Formerly blond hairs were now matted with a putrid gray slime. His delightful discovery was a large decomposed lake trout that had been lying on the beach for several weeks. The stench was so overpowering that it triggered an instant retching reflex. Everyone expressed revulsion at the sickening smell—everyone that is—except Beau Jo. He stood in front of me with tail wagging an entire body and a happy expression that seemed to say, "Hey boss, you should be happy now. I no longer smell like a skunk."

He could not be convinced that the second smell was much worse than the first. Nor could he understand why I gingerly tied him to a tree in front of our cottage that afternoon and used high-pressure spray from a hose nozzle to dislodge the scum from his body. It was only then that the tomato juice, which eventually neutralized the skunk odor, could be applied.

Cover-up, a story of a dog's vain effort to hide one odor with another that was even worse. How much simpler it would have been had he bypassed the decayed fish and instead let me apply the tomato juice. Yet how typical of human reaction when faced with a similar situation. We are all guilty to one degree or another.

Even one so mighty as a king anointed by God succumbed. David's seduction of Uriah's wife, Bathsheba, and the events that followed are recorded in 2 Samuel 11 and 12. Her message, "I am pregnant," that followed their tryst sent King David scurrying in pursuit of a cover-up, with the murder of Uriah the ultimate attempt. David thought that the odor of his initial transgression had been obliterated. It took the prophet Nathan's confrontational "You are the man!" (2 Samuel 12:7a) to make David aware of the stench of his sin. How simple it would have been had he placed his original transgression in God's hands and waited there for His cleansing.

Cover-up! It has led to the resignation of a president, wars between nations, murders of innocent victims, and betrayal of marriage partners. No one is immune. It is one of the fruits of our sinful nature manifesting itself in selfishness. Our instinctive reaction when caught in wrongdoing is to let someone else take the blame. It may be as small as a white lie or as major as perjury, but the result is always the same. The stench of cover up is a thousand times worse than the odor of the initial transgression.

Remember Beau Jo? There is a divine counterpart to the tomato juice that finally removed his offensive aroma—the blood of Christ. God promises that it obliterates the stench of every sin. It is our Savior, Jesus Christ, who has provided the ultimate cleansing. As we kneel before Him, He cleanses us in the waters of Baptism and restores us through His body and blood. Then He places on our shoulders the one garment that can cover our darkest misdeed—the cloak of Christ's righteousness. With lives washed clean and enveloped in sanctification, we are welcomed into His presence and taken into His arms. What a cover-up!

If we confess our sins, He is faithful and just and will forgive us our sins and purify us from all unrighteousness. 1 John 1:9

THE EVERLASTING ARMS

Lynn and I had received the invitation to her nursing class reunion at the home of a classmate. Our journey took us to a small ranch in Montana. There, a spacious home was nestled in the flank of a rocky hillside. The location offered a commanding view of the sprawling Bitterroot River valley situated a few miles to the west. It was a setting that defined the word "peace."

Adding to the sense of tranquility was the gurgling sound of water flowing in a nearby irrigation canal. Designed by early pioneers, it had been meticulously carved from the steep slopes by the calloused hands and aching muscles of determined laborers. It was created to guide life-giving waters on a 60-mile journey from Lake Como to the arid soil of the valley floor. It would have been difficult for those laborers to envision the beauty of a lush irrigated flatland now tucked against the towering heights of the brooding Bitterroot Mountains.

The early morning hours found me, camera in hand, eagerly picking my way along the rock-strewn bank of the stream. My companions were solitude and contentment. The only disturbance of the silence was the occasional click of the shutter. A peace engulfed my senses—until it was shattered by a mallard's clamorous alarm-call.

Startled, I turned my head so my eyes could focus on the source of this vocal invasion. There, just a few yards upstream, was a mother duck desperately trying to entice her young brood to gather under her protective custody. Within seconds 10 fragile downy balls had instinctively formed an oval raft that tucked itself beneath the shadow of her tail. Diminutive legs mimicked the mother's strong stroke as they moved in perfect formation across the current toward a sheltered cove in the opposite bank.

But a tragedy seemed to be in the making. One duckling had become separated from the group and was now in midstream. Struggling to survive, it battled the tumbling current that was threatening to sweep it away. Tiny webbed feet paddled furiously, at times lifting its fuzzy frame from the surface of the stream, but to no avail. Without a mother's body to deflect the relentless energy of the flowing waters, the forces of nature were slowly beginning to have their way. My heart yearned to reach out and cup my hands around this unfortunate newborn, but I was too far away from the struggle. It quickly became apparent that this helpless infant was doomed.

Then it happened! Some instinct prompted Mom Duck to realize that one of her brood was missing, even though a jutting bank hid the silent struggle of her offspring from her view. Suddenly reversing course, she courageously turned and again braved the strong flow. Midway across, she turned downstream—all the while trailing her raft of tiny dependents.

The powerful thrust of webbed feet devoured the distance in seconds. As she approached the frantic infant, she turned upstream with timing so perfect that the lost one was swallowed up within the friendly confines of 10 sibling bodies. In an instant, the unity of the flock had been restored. How I wish I could have understood the murmuring and comforting cheeps coming from that tiny entourage as she escorted them back upstream to the sanctuary of the cove.

That drama of nature could be a reflection of human life. There have been times when I, like that duckling, have become separated from the flock. I have lived through moments when the rushing waters of life seemed to overpower me and the swift currents of adversity threatened to sweep me away to destruction.

We all encounter days when it seems that, no matter how hard we struggle, our best efforts are insufficient to keep us abreast of the current. It may be a life-threatening or debilitating illness. Sometimes financial worries are the culprit. Family problems can wear us down. A job is lost or fails to live up to expectations. Perhaps it is simply the routines and pressures of daily life. Like the duckling, we feel deserted, out of control, and seemingly beyond retrieval.

Yet there is One who does not forget. No matter how overwhelmed we may feel, there is a Father who is aware of our situation. Three beautiful parables of Jesus are recorded in Luke 15 for the benefit of those struggling to escape the current. In simple language, He described a lost sheep, a lost coin, and a lost son, all to illustrate our Father's concern for each of us. It was God who promised Joshua that "I will never leave you nor forsake you" (Joshua 1:5). Jesus extends a similar assurance to you and me in Matthew 28:20, "Surely I am with you always, to the very end of the age."

How I treasure those changeless promises from Almighty God! They are so precious that I have stored them in my heart and engraved them on my mind. But how does He fulfill them? Does He reach down physically from heaven so His arms actually enfold us? The mother duck did not take the duckling in her bill and carry it to safety or place it on her back where it could nestle among her feathers. She maneuvered her entourage so the raft of siblings became the protective arms while she used the strength of her body to deflect the rushing waters.

So it is with our great God! He who could command legions of angels to surround us instead whispers a reassuring message: "My son, My daughter. I know what is troubling you. In Me you will find the strength to deflect the current. You will be encircled by those I bring to you."

There have been moments when God used the arms of family or the fellowship of believers, friends, to encircle me in a warm blanket of love. There also have been days when I reached out to embrace and comfort others. No matter what the circumstances, I have never been alone in my struggle—and neither will you!

That promise will be mine even during that hour "When ends life's transient dream, when death's cold, sullen stream, Rolls over me. ..." I know that Jesus will be there, swimming toward me through the dark water. At exactly the right moment He will turn and—as He breaks the current—will encircle me with a raft of saints who already live in His presence. What a joyful reunion that will be as our Savior leads us to that sheltering cove on the opposite bank where we will spend an eternity in God's presence.

This promise of rescue that was fulfilled in a humble manger in the tiny town of Bethlehem and on a crude cross at the crest of a hill called Calvary. It is a promise revealed by Almighty God to all believers. It is a promise that is bestowed upon us at our Baptism and renewed in the Sacrament of the Altar. It is a promise that is ours for all eternity.

The eternal God is your refuge, and underneath are the everlasting arms. Deuteronomy 33:27a

THE GENTLE TOUCH

The summer sun, launching a savage assault from its zenith, struggled to penetrate the leafy barrier protecting the occupants of the park. Welcome balmy breezes wandered through the tree-studded environs, cooling the human and canine tenants gathered there for the annual kennel club all-breed dog show.

The center of the activity was a building housing the judging rings. Before long our granddaughter and I had worked our way inside, eagerly wandering from one area to another. Occasionally we would cheer on our favorites among the various classes of dogs being evaluated. It was a fence-enclosed arena bearing the sign "Obedience Trials," however, that lured us back time and again. Anxious contestants stood nearby, clustered according to experience.

The initial judging concentrated on individual performance. Trainers demanded unquestioning obedience while issuing a set of commands that included heel, sit, fetch, jump, and stay. The group trial that followed was the ultimate test of staying power. Owners led the dogs into the ring and arranged them in a ragged line-abreast formation. Each handler snapped the order "Sit!" quickly followed by "Stay!" They then walked out of the ring and out of eyesight of their canine charge. Each dog's test was to mimic a statue for the tedious eight minutes that elapsed before the boss would return.

Occupying the end position in the line was Jalk, a magnificent German shepherd. His ears stood at attention as his trainer departed, but soon dropped as boredom set in. Within four minutes, he had slouched to his stomach, there to remain until the return of a highly displeased owner.

A brief walk in a tight circle, a return to the lineup, sharp commands "Down!" "Stay!" and the dozen dogs were in prone positions. Again the monotonous wait. Yet within two minutes Jalk started creeping forward, his belly scraping the ground. Bit by bit he inched his way across the ring. Finally the judge had to grab the leash and restrain him for the final moments.

A clearly disappointed master did not even enter the ring. His biting order to "Come" was obeyed by a dog whose tucked tail and collapsed ears testified of his shame. He sat before the one he had failed with head bowed as he awaited the punishment so richly deserved.

I watched intently, expecting to witness a severe tongue-lashing. Instead, to my utter disbelief, the owner reached down and, gently cupping the dog's head in his hands, softly said, "That's okay, Jalk. We'll do better next time." The nose and tongue of the grateful recipient of unexpected forgiveness thoroughly moistened the extended fingers of his master's hand.

In that instant I saw my relationship to God. My daily acts of selfish disobedience are deserving of anger. Yet His response is always one of a gentle touch and a whispered phrase, "That's okay. We'll do better next time!"

This assurance of a new beginning comes to me—and all Christians—as a gift, purchased through the sinless life, painful death, and glorious resurrection of the Son of God. Because of the daily washing of our sins, we can rejoice in the restored relationship to our Master.

The LORD is compassionate and gracious, slow to anger, abounding in love. ... He does not treat us as our sins deserve or repay us according to our iniquities. For as high as the heavens are above the earth, so great is His love for those who fear Him; as far as the east is from the west, so far has He removed our transgressions from us. Psalm 103:8, 10–12

I'LL DO IT MY WAY!

A popular Frank Sinatra ballad of long ago was titled "My Way." It is easy to understand why the words of a song from a bygone era still grab our attention. From the earliest days of infancy, our inherited selfish nature makes "doing it my way" the dominant theme of our lives. That is especially true when we resist God, directing our own activities. It took two tiny creatures to bring that to my attention in a unique way.

It was early summer, and the brief stroll along the lakeshore provided a welcome respite from the challenges of managing a camp bursting at the seams with families seeking a week of spiritual renewal. Reflections of a brilliant afternoon sun danced across the crests of tumbling waves in patterns choreographed by God to sooth my troubled spirit. The crunch of moistened sand, compressed beneath unfettered toes, mingled with the hypnotic ebb and flow of restless waters to create an atmosphere of unspeakable peace.

As I meandered along the beach, my gaze was captured by a flurry of activity. Directly before me, in a miniature arena formed by a footprint, were two Lilliputian gladiators engaged in a life-and-death struggle. One was a black wasp, the other a molting sand crab that had just shed its protective armor. The latter held delicate claws erect in a defensive posture, attempting to use its size advantage to parry the deadly thrusts of the opponent's venomous rapier.

Although the defensive efforts were valiant, the skirmish was brief. One lightning-like thrust of the slender black abdomen, one drop of paralyzing potion injected into the vulnerable naked body, and it was over. The triumphant wasp waited patiently as the movements of a vanquished foe became erratic, and then ceased.

"To the victor belong the spoils," I thought. "Let the feast begin!" I lingered nearby, wondering just how he would dispose of this delicate morsel. To my surprise the wasp immediately clamped its mandibles around one of the pink claws. Then, with leg movement thrown into reverse and flailing wildly, he moved slowly backward while dragging the crab out of the depression and across the sandy beach. Somehow he managed to steer a string-straight course toward the eroded edge of a nearby sand dune.

It was the trilogy of direction, devotion, and duty that finally gave me the insight necessary to grasp the significance of the drama I was witnessing. This was a female wasp, not a male as I had presumptuously thought, and she was in the process of acquiring the perfect egg repository. The carcass she was determined to move would shelter the fragile eggs and then provide an initial food supply for the newly emerged larvae.

One task remained. Somehow she knew that if the body and the precious embryos were to remain safe, they had to be deposited above the highest level of storm-induced wave action. With wings lacking the lifting power for air transport, she was reduced to dragging a body five times her size across the loose sand. It was the equivalent of diminutive David dragging giant Goliath across the Sahara. For me the distance equaled one short stride. For her it was an endless wasteland to be conquered inch by painful inch.

Before long I became sympathetic to her cause and caught up in her ambitious undertaking. Because of my height I could survey the entire scene at a single glance. It became obvious that there was an easy solution to her struggle. "Why not," I reasoned to myself, "take a long stem of sea oats and use it to gently push the crab from the rear. That will accelerate her progress by reducing the resistance. The length of the stalk plus her limited intelligence will preclude associating me with the push. As a result, she should be overwhelmed by gratitude and relief as her burden is eased."

I bent over and, with the long slim stem held at the end of my outstretched arm, cautiously applied pressure. The decrease in resistance brought an instant response, but it was not the appreciation I anticipated; rather it was a display of intense rage. I stumbled backward with hands lifted to shield my face as she angrily buzzed around my head. A minute went by before she returned to her labors. Apparently my motionless figure no longer posed a threat.

A short while later the ceaseless tugging had brought her face-to-face with a new challenge. She had reached the point where the level surface of the beach met the eroded face of the dune. Sand crumbled and slid downward beneath the pressure of her slender legs. Every inch forward was followed by a half-inch backward slide. It was apparent that reaching her goal without outside help would be difficult at best.

Still struggling with an overwhelming desire to help, I found several thin pieces of driftwood and carefully pressed them into the sand along her projected path. It worked! Reaching the first, she scrambled up over the edge onto the smooth surface. There the solid footing enabled her to swiftly progress to the top and, unfortunately, also off the end. Unaware of my carefully laid-out plan, she set out on a new course that failed to intercept the second strip of wood. It was akin to sliding off the interstate while driving across the Mojave Desert. She was again floundering in the sand.

Still desiring to be helpful, I gently moved the next "highway" into her path. The resulting slight tremor triggered an instinctive reaction. In her eyes this was the return of an earlier intruder who must once more be repulsed to protect her prize. An immediate attack was launched with my head again the prime target. I beat a hasty retreat as she circled at ear level.

When her wings brushed my nose in a gesture of defiance, I slowed my movements to reduce possibility of deployment of her ultimate weapon. I did not relish the thought of venom deposited beneath my skin! A brief touchdown on the top of my hair conveyed an unmistakable "stay away" before she returned to her self-appointed task.

Acknowledging defeat, I watched from a distance as she again began her arduous labors. I felt frustrated and disappointed as I thought of her refusal to accept my assistance. What could have been minutes of minimal effort was hours of intense struggle. I returned to camp discouraged by my inability to communicate, yet I nurtured a hope that she had overcome the obstacles and achieved her goal.

That chance encounter with nature showed me that

I am often in the role of a wasp struggling ineffectively with a burden while at the same time resisting all offers of divine assistance. Standing at the side is a heavenly Father watching my feeble efforts.

He sees me trying to overcome obstacles for which detours and bridges have already been built. He longs to reach out and gently nudge a load that exhausts my limited resources but is minute when measured against His strength. His one desire is to help me reach my goal. And what is my reaction? Blind and possessive as the wasp, I repeat again and again "I'll do it my way!"

God sees my feet slipping and sliding while I try to move a boulder labeled "Worry about the Future." Reaching out with His Word, He gently pushes against the rock with the promise; "So do not worry, saying, 'What shall we eat?' or 'What shall we drink?' or 'What shall we wear?' For the pagans run after all these things, and your heavenly Father knows that you need them" (Matthew 6:31–32). He paves the path with the reassurance, "Do not be anxious about anything, but in everything, by prayer and petition, with thanksgiving, present your requests to God. And the peace of God, which transcends all understanding, will guard your hearts and minds in Christ Jesus" (Philippians 4:6–7).

But as the wasp erroneously thought she was protecting her prize, so I covet my possessions and place my trust in that which I own. When God nudges my efforts to redirect my path by suggesting that "Each one should use whatever gift he has received to serve others" (1 Peter 4:10a), I express my irritation by lashing out to protect that which I think I own. But thanks be to God that He is loving, merciful, and long-suffering.

I walked away from the wasp frustrated, discouraged, and powerless. But God never leaves my side nor stops helping me. When I fail to understand, He sends the Holy Spirit to clear my vision, and He covers me with the forgiveness that is mine through Christ's body and blood. Through His power, I am gradually learning to shift the burden and relinquish control. The wisdom of His gentle words "Be still, and know that I am God"(Psalm 46:10a), is becoming more apparent every day.

I wish I could have done the same for the wasp.

JONATHAN

The storm that had battered our lakeside family retreat center the night before displayed the type of ferocity that can be expected as the aftermath of a hot muggy day in late July. The facility was filled to capacity, and most of the guests had spent a major portion of the previous evening enthralled by the spectacular display of the Creator's power. The thundering surf of Lake Michigan, illuminated in bursts of horizon-spanning lightning, had lapped hungrily at the seawall. Even the trees had bowed their heads in humble submission to the power of the forces that assailed them.

The rays of the morning sun, unobstructed in an atmosphere washed clean, dispelled any fears left over from the preceding hours. Few could resist the beckoning beach, now bordered by placid waters reflecting the delph-blue sky, and its treasure-trove of storm-deposited debris. Bare feet, bent heads, and searching eyes quickly became the order of the day.

I was working on the patio, enjoying the warmth of the midday sun, when a guest rushed up and informed me of a find she had just made. Leading me to the water's edge, she pointed to a seagull that had, from all outward appearances, succumbed to the ferocity of the storm. Its head hung limp as I picked up the water-soaked body. Apparently the natural waterproofing had been lost, causing the unfortunate bird to loose buoyancy and drown.

Thoughts of a quick burial were interrupted as we saw a slight movement of its beak coupled with a barely discernable gasp for breath. A spark of life still existed, and that was enough to spur us on to action! Applying principles of human CPR to waterfowl physique, the body was suspended head down while the breast was gently compressed in a rhythmic movement. The technique was crude but the results were positive. Fluid flowing from the beak indicated that lungs were draining, and soon the spasmodic gasps for air came with increasing regularity.

The blazing afternoon sun soon dried the soggy plumage of the helpless bird lying cradled in a towel on the leeward side of a building. The penetrating rays also fanned the spark of life smoldering within its breast. By evening eyelids were half-open and the throat rattle had subsided.

With the unexpected recovery came another problem—restoring the strength of our helpless patient. Since this was a first-time experience, the diet was determined with little or no knowledge of principles of ornithology. Fish, the natural food, could not be swallowed. Cod liver oil appeared to be a viable substitute, which, after being mixed with liquid dog vitamins, was administered with an eyedropper.

The evening chill dictated a move to a box in our bedroom with warmth supplied by a suspended light bulb. I spent a night of fitful slumber interrupted by frequent trips between our bed and the nearby A.I.C.U. (Aviary Intensive Care Unit). The few drops of sustenance administered during each visit appeared to have a positive effect. By morning the seagull could lift its head momentarily.

By now the condition of our rescued storm victim was the center of conversation among the guests. Detailed "bulletins" were issued after each meal. In addition, many made at least one tiptoe visit to the gull, by now named "Jonathan," to personally wish him a speedy recovery. He responded by doing just that. By the end of the second day, the gull was able to swallow the oil-enriched canned sardines that were placed in his beak. On the fourth day, he took his first swim in our half-filled bathtub and ate a few of the minnows floating on the surface.

As Jonathan's vigor returned, it became apparent that a move from the A.I.C.U. to a C.C.F. (Continuing Care Facility) was necessary. A small outdoor pen with four-foot high snowfence walls was constructed to accommodate him. It was complete with a log perch and private pond. This became his home for the remainder of his stay.

As I carefully nursed Jonathan back to health, I began to imagine that a bond was being established between the airborne and earthbound. "Surely," I thought, "he will recognize that his restored life is largely the result of my efforts, and will therefore display some form of gratitude." I could even picture him perched contentedly on my shoulder while guests marveled at this unique relationship.

What an impossible dream that turned out to be. In fact, just the opposite seemed to be true. Feeding time became a war of nerves. The preferred fresh smelt would be accepted only if held before his beak. Yet holding it in my hand also meant that I would get bitten. Even extending my reach by impaling the morsel on the end of a short stick gave no assurance of safety. He was just as apt to make a lightning-fast stab at the nearest part of my anatomy as he was to grasp the meal.

Jonathan quickly became a popular member of our Saturday evening staff talent show. His initial stage presentation was billed as a mysterious object contained in a cardboard box that I held. After an adequate buildup, I would reach inside the box and securely fasten my hands around his wings. He would then be brought into view to face an enthralled audience, the majority of whom were getting their first close-up look at a herring gull.

They may have listened with rapt attention to my dramatic description of the rescue and recovery of Jonathan, but my thoughts were directed elsewhere. My eyes were fixed on that yellow beak terminating in a needle-sharp hook. I hoped to somehow avoid the nip he seemed determined to administer.

My monologue was delivered with a "The Show Must Go On" attitude that gave no hint of the pain erupting from the fold of skin on my arm slowly being pierced by the gull's unrelenting pressure. All the while his yellow eyes glared defiantly without the slightest indication of fear.

There was an air of fierce independence about Jonathan that formed an insurmountable wall of separation. It was a quality that initially caused a feeling of frustration but which was eventually transformed into admiration. Domestication was not part of his plan. Rather it seemed that freedom was his one desire, even if it meant losing an ample supply of fish and protective care. Every meal was followed by a wing-flapping exercise, and each day found him rising a bit higher above his log perch.

There finally came a day in late August when a strong north wind combined with flailing feathers to provide the lift necessary to surmount the fence. I watched as he slowly gained altitude on his course toward the lake. Within minutes he was one among many. In my imagination I could almost see him gather his winged companions about to tell them about "the strange creatures I met who had not yet learned to fly." It was equally easy to picture him describing, "the big nest at the edge of the lake in which they live and where I once resided."

My thoughts often turned to Jonathan in the days that followed, especially in regard to all the loving care that had been lavished upon him. "Why would he want to return to the harsh conditions of the wild," I asked myself, "and leave behind the carefree life I was willing to provide for him? Didn't he realize that my only desire had been for his good, that his rescue from certain death was due only to my persistent efforts? How could he be so ungrateful?"

It was during one of these self-indulgent sessions that I began to realize that my attitude toward my heavenly Father differed little from that exhibited by Jonathan toward me.

How similar my initial condition had been to his.

Tossed about by storms and engulfed in sin, I was powerless to save myself. All spiritual life had left my body as I lay helpless on the "beach" of human existence. The "feathers" of my free will, soaked by the selfishness of my corrupt natural desires, were incapable of lifting me to higher levels. From all outward appearances, death was a certain destiny.

Such it would have been had Christ not come, spotted me lying among the debris of my sin, and reached down with arms of love to lift me to Himself. A spark of hope was restored through the powerful ministrations of the Holy Spirit. "Feathers," cleansed by the blood of Christ, were dried in the warmth of God's love. A "Gospel diet," prepared and administered under the guidance of the Holy Spirit, gradually gave me spiritual strength.

None of this would be possible had God not intervened. Everything good comes from His hand. He stands at my side, ready to meet my every need in such a way that my life can be filled with love, joy, and peace. He has promised that I need never again hunger and thirst because I can partake of the banquet He has prepared for me. Furthermore, I have tasted His food, tried His promises, and know that everything He says is true!

Why then do I, like Jonathan, rebel? Why do I still crave independence, seek to satisfy my needs by my own abilities, believe that I know what is best for me? Why am I so quick, when things go wrong, to snap at the hand that feeds me—and so slow, when my world seems rosy and bright, to express gratitude? Am I really so different from the herring gull who so often frustrated and angered me and who, in the end, flew out of my grasp?

How similar are my actions to those demonstrated by Jonathan, and how dissimilar God's reactions are to mine! True, I think I can imagine the hurt He feels and the tears He sheds as a result of my rebellion. I can almost sense His frustration as I ignore the joy-filled path He has laid out before me and insist on finding my own way. What I cannot begin to understand or appreciate is His response.

Instead of anger, I find forgiveness. Rather than pushing me down, He picks me up. His open hand is filled with gifts that are freely offered but never forced on me. Sometimes I reject His generosity and instead embark upon flights of my own making that end in disaster. Even then He has never once abandoned me. His helping and healing hand has always been ready to replace broken feathers and to restore torn muscles. And no matter how often or hard I try, He never lets me fly beyond His reach. He knows me and brings me back, even when I mingle with flock of this world, and again places me within the enclosure of His love.

The raucous cry of a gull flying overhead was a common occurrence in the tiny Michigan community where we once lived, yet that sound will never become commonplace to my ear. I whisper a prayer of thanks to my Lord for permitting a feathered friend to come into my life. Through that lowly creature, He enriched my spiritual life and enhanced my vision and appreciation of our Father's love.

I know that nothing good lives in me, that is, in my sinful nature. ... What a wretched man I am! Who will rescue me from this body of death? Thanks be to God—through Jesus Christ our Lord! Romans 7:18, 24–25

But those who hope in the LORD will renew their strength. They will soar on wings like eagles; they will run and not grow weary, they will walk and not be faint. Isaiah 40:31

MIRACLES DON'T HAPPEN?

"I must give him a bath before we drop him off. We want him to look his best when Mabel's guests arrive." We were in the throes of completing last minute "must do's" prior to our evening departure for London, and topping the list was delivering our cocker spaniel, Beau Jo, to his home-away-from-home.

It was December. I had just completed my first quarter as Dean of Student Affairs at a teachers college and was eagerly anticipating a respite from the tension-laced responsibilities of that position. Our youngest daughter's wedding was scheduled for December 20 in her fiancé's ancestral hometown of Hollywell Green in Yorkshire, England. Needless to say, Lynn and I were energized as we faced our daughter's wedding and our first civilian excursion to a foreign land.

Mabel lived six miles north of our Chicago apartment with heavily traveled Harlem Avenue the most direct route. My impatience with traffic lights prompted me to add four miles to the journey by going out of my way to avoid the busy route. Still damp from his bath, Beau Jo was exhausted from his struggle to retain his cherished doggie odor and spent the half-hour snoozing near the heater vent in the passenger compartment.

All of that changed when he heard the welcoming voice of his favorite caretaker, for embodied in those dulcet tones was the promise of a warm lap and endless snacks. We gave her his collar and the attached tags that were to be put on after his coat dried. Fond farewells went unnoticed by an erstwhile canine companion totally captivated by intriguing odors emanating from the kitchen.

The following eight days were crammed with the myriad activities of the wedding, sightseeing, and new experiences. Museums, ancient castles, crown jewels, and royal pageantry became part of a tapestry woven with images of a marriage ceremony in an English village whose birth date preceded the Pilgrims' journey.

At the end of our trip, we emerged from the jet way with eyes searching for Mabel's joyous welcome. Instead, we gathered into our arms a body wracked with sobs and heard a voice struggle to whisper the anguished words, "Beau Jo is lost!" It was 10 minutes before she regained sufficient composure to explain.

Everything had gone well on the first day until Beau

Jo begged to go out for one final stroll in the fenced backyard before retiring for the night. He dashed out the back door that Mabel had opened and, to her horror, continued on through a gate that someone had left ajar. Lying on the table was a collar and the attached identity tags. She ran out to the street calling his name, but her beautiful blond friend had disappeared into the inky darkness. The remainder of the night was spent driving through the neighborhood in vain hope that he might be found.

I still shudder when trying to imagine the intensity of the anguish and guilt she endured during that week of waiting for our return. The area dog pounds received daily visits. Local police and animal control officers were asked to report dead dogs fitting Beau Jo's description. Ads were placed in the local newspapers. All avenues had been pursued. All produced uniform negative results. Beau Jo remained among the missing.

Gloom enshrouded the Christmas family gathering several days later. The one who had joined our ranks as a Christmas gift nine years earlier and quickly wormed his way into our collective hearts had disappeared from our midst. Gone were the gorgeous brown eyes and wagging tail that could extract a tasty morsel from an adamant Scrooge. In its place rested the image of a lost and frightened dog searching for a familiar face and friendly hand.

Our newly wedded daughter joined us later that week for a final all-out assault. The neighborhood surrounding Mabel's home was blanketed with handbills. Doorbells were rung. Ads were renewed. Rewards were offered. Local pounds were visited. Nothing bore fruit.

The first sub-zero temperatures of winter arrived four weeks after Beau Jo ventured through the open gate. Thoughts naturally turned to him as I lay in bed that Sunday night, huddled beneath layers of blankets to ward off the cold. Tears filled my eyes as I envisioned a shivering dog with bleeding paws frantically seeking shelter from the Arctic blasts. "Please, Lord," I prayed, "lead me to discover his fate so the burden of this terrible uncertainty might be lifted from my shoulders. It is destroying my inner peace."

The next morning I was headed for the office when the phone rang. My impatience was evident as I handed the receiver to Lynn after hearing the familiar words, "Is this the party that is searching for information about a lost dog?" The offer of a reward had prompted a number of futile calls, each adding to the heap of dashed hopes. But as I walked toward the door I detected a different tone in my wife's voice. Instead of the usual "No," I heard her respond with one "Yes" after another. By the time I returned to the phone it was evident that Beau Jo had been found and was in the care of the woman who was calling.

Thoughts of office obligations were shoved aside by the surge of excitement we experienced while driving across town to the address Lynn had received. We sounded the doorbell and in response heard a bark that made our scalp tingle. We waited impatiently while the door slowly opened. There stood a woman with three dogs vying for the right to greet these visitors. As I knelt on the threshold a blond bomb burst from the trio and catapulted itself into my arms. A split second later a familiar pink tongue was working non-stop to remove the salty rivulets running down my cheeks. Beau Jo was back!

We spent the next 30 minutes sharing and reliving the events of the past three weeks. One half-hour later we carried the newly found escapee into the first grade classroom where a surprised Mabel was teaching. It is impossible to describe the joy of that reunion and to see and hear her expression of relief as a ton of guilt and remorse was lifted from her shoulders.

The lost dog saga bordered on the unbelievable. His rescuer was a widow who had driven 10 miles west through a chilling drizzle one Sunday morning to visit her husband's grave. On departing, she stopped at the grocery store across the highway. Huddled in the entryway was a soaked, shivering, and exhausted dog desperately searching for a bit of warmth. The newsboy standing nearby indicated that the dog had been there since early in the morning. She immediately became concerned about his well-being while also recognizing the apparent quality of his breeding. Her compassionate reaction was to wrap a willing dog in a warm blanket and tenderly carry him to her car.

How (and why) had he made his way to that store? Apparently Beau Jo had one thought in mind when he ran through the gate, and that was to return to our apartment. Relying on instinct, he retraced the exact route we had driven the day before, although he had slumbered on the floor through the entire trip. Somehow he crossed the busy expressway during the wee morning hours and was within four miles of his destination when aching feet and a bone-chilling fatigue brought his wild journey to a momentary halt. The inviting entrance provided a welcome respite. Fortunately the woman found him before he could return to our apartment where he thought we would be.

Despite experiencing love at first sight, this kind woman's overarching desire was to return the dog she now called "Buddy" to his rightful owners. She faced a daunting task because of the complete lack of identification. (His collar was still at Mabel's.) Giving up would have been understandable. Yet she continued to search area newspapers for some clue to his identity and his owners.

Unfortunately, our search had been concentrated in

a different suburb and our detailed ads were placed in different newspapers. The final "desperation ad" ran in the metropolitan paper that particular Sunday. An illness kept this dog lover from working on Monday. This bonus of extra time presented her with an opportunity to thoroughly review the lost dog ads and somehow connect our description with her Buddy.

There have been a number of times in my life when God's answer to a specific prayer was so evident that I could almost feel His presence. Such was the case on that cold January morning. As we drove back to the campus, I was not only overwhelmed by a sense of gratitude for all that God had done, but was also led again to recognize His unique character. How wonderful to know and worship a God so powerful that the forces of nature obey His commands yet so loving that He hears and answers the prayers of one of His children who is concerned about a dog.

I have relived that morning many times in the years since and I have been led to the following conclusion:

God used an incident that began with human error (the gate left open) to help accomplish His purpose in two completely unrelated areas. For you see, God's response to my prayer had wider implications.

First, our campus was embroiled in a conflict that was on the verge of tearing apart our community. At the center was the refusal to renew the contract of a popular professor. My renewed awareness of God's presence, demonstrated in His love for me, led me to new strength and courage. On the following day I asked a friend to join me in fervent prayer, asking God to somehow influence certain minds to do the unthinkable—reverse a firm decision. On Wednesday morning an announcement was made in chapel that the contract would be renewed. I still cry when I think of that moment when God's power and love was again revealed as peace was restored to our campus.

The second effect was a further demonstration of God's omnipresent love. The throat ailment of the woman who found Beau Jo was ultimately diagnosed as carcinoma of the larynx. Our newly formed relationship permitted Lynn and me to share with her the Gospel message of Christ's redemption and to minister to her spiritual needs during the final year of her life. She believed and today she enjoys the joy of heaven—all because a gate was left open so long ago.

Have you seen God at work in your life? He's there. Come meet Him in worship. Ponder His love poured out upon you through Christ. Listen for Him in His Word. And look around you. Sometimes the love that our heavenly Father showers upon His children is revealed in unexplainable ways. Keep your eyes open—it could be happening to you.

Miracles Don't Happen?

"Miracles don't happen—
at least not in this day.

We know so much 'bout many things,"
I've heard some people say,

"We've looked inside the atom,
and traveled into space

What once was supernatural is now just
commonplace."

Miracles don't happen? Then sit with me,
my friend

And listen to a tale of woe that has a happy
end.

Our hero is a cocker span',
a dog of vintage nine

His name is Beau combined with Jo, his hair as
blond as mine.

It happened last December,
ten days before the Yule

In a city known as "windy" where the air was
more than cool.

Beau had remained behind with friends while
Mom and Dad flew east,

Ten miles he was from home that night,
long miles to say the least.

'Twas shortly after midnight when he walked
out through the door

With one thought on his mind, I guess,

to get back home once more.

All sights and sounds were strange to him;
no friendly hand was near,

His heart was pounding frantically; his eyes
were filled with fear.

Westward he raced for many a mile to a
street we drove that day

One he had never seen before—how could
he know that way?

Yet there he turned and headed south as
though he had a map,

Explain that one to me, my friend, to earn
your thinking cap.

Six miles he ran before he paused to rest his
aching feet

And there a woman came to him,
a woman kind and sweet

Who wrapped him in the warmth of love
and took him home that day

He had no tags—his name not known—
he found a place to stay.

Four weeks went by with in-between a
Christmas bleak and sad

And then one day a phone call came,
in answer to an ad,

The last day it was running, a woman
home from work

Had time to read that paper—don't call it
just a quirk.

*You may not see a miracle bound in this
epilogue*

*But I see God with open arms concerned
about a dog!*

*And if God has that kind of love for crea-
tures weak and small*

*Then how much more must He love you,
most precious of them all.*

*Of that the angels sang one night,
while shepherds bended low*

*For Christ, God's Son,
had come to earth so many years ago.*

*He came for you, to bring you rest,
forgiveness for your sin,*

*Through the waters' splash in Baptism,
the miracle begins.*

*The miracle's for everyone;
I know it to be true*

*Peace, joy, and life eternal,
He offers these to you.*

*How great is the love the Father has lavished on us, that
we should be called children of God! And that is what we are!*
1 John 3:1a

THE MOUSE THAT WOULD NOT QUIT

The rays of a bright October sun, hanging high in the afternoon sky, penetrated our clothes to warm our skin. Daughter Sherry and I were struggling to reduce a narrow, five-foot high rank of wood to a length acceptable to our demanding woodstove. Chips flew as the snarling teeth of the chainsaw tore at the resisting fibers, quickly severing one from the other.

The work flowed smoothly until the removal of a key block of wood brought the face of the stack tumbling down. The scattering chunks of wood forced a pause in our labors as we contemplated our next move. The brief break was welcome, for arms and backs were beginning to ache from the bending and lifting. However, it was more than fatigue that caused us to completely forget what we had been doing. Our focus turned instead to the drama unfolding before us.

On center stage was the shattered remnant of a nest

among the disarray of fallen timber. The principal players appeared to be three baby mice, huddled in the ruins of what had been a carefully constructed hollow ball of shredded leaves and dried grass. Their tiny bodies, angry in the pink and gray of their nakedness, were instinctively huddled together as protection against the autumn chill. Our hearts ached as we viewed their helplessness and we wanted to somehow make amends for the violence that had befallen them. The question was one of translating our longings into reality.

A faint rustling in the covering of the forest floor near our feet shifted the focus of our attention. There, silhouetted against a fallen autumn leaf, was a deer mouse. But she was not alone! Suspended from her tiny jaws was the submissive body of one of her offspring, grasped securely by the nape of the neck. Scrambling over the six-inch deep layer of leaves, she set course for another woodpile 20 feet away. The numerous openings she saw gave promise of shelter.

We mentally marked the point where she entered her new abode, then tenderly transported the cup-shaped remnant with its three trembling occupants to that location. Within moments the mother came out to investigate and then, one by one, carried the diminutive bodies of her offspring into their new home.

Our plan to return to our labors was again interrupted by the sight of the mouse bounding vigorously over the leaves in our direction. Was she abandoning the young she had just labored so valiantly to rescue? I moved my booted foot in an attempt to force her to reverse her course. To our surprise, she did not flinch, even when dwarfed by the menacing approach of the boot tip. Instead, she rushed past on her way to the spot where the nest had fallen. Several minutes elapsed as disturbed leaves gave evidence of her passage. Then she emerged and dashed toward her distant newfound home, clutching in her jaws yet another product of her womb.

"This should be it," I said to Sherry, "five is the usual litter size." Therefore, her unexpected return caught us by surprise.

"Maybe she is going to gather nesting material," I said as she scrambled up the craggy face of the rank of wood awaiting our attention. For the next five minutes we observed her progress through the maze of passages separating the loosely piled blocks. Up and down—side-to-side—there was an air of frantic haste in her movements. Finally she emerged, proudly carrying—yes, you guessed it—number six! It was in record time that she traversed the long, obstacle-strewn path she had earlier blazed, and then reappeared no more. Her family was again intact; the last one had been found and was safe in the nest.

How did she know there were six offspring?

Counting would appear to be beyond the capability of mouse intellect. I cannot answer that question, but I do know that we had witnessed an act of courage and devotion. We had been in the presence of a mother willing to sacrifice her very life to save her young.

I was overwhelmed by emotion as I contemplated the wonder of what we had just seen. And in the warmth of that moment, I saw myself as I had once been—as helpless as the infant mouse in that shattered nest.

I thought of the story of creation and the "nest" God created in the Garden of Eden to house an infant human race. It was designed as a sheltering environment where Adam and Eve would live forever in peace and harmony. Unfortunately they succumbed to a carefully planned satanic temptation. In the aftermath, the "nest" was shattered beyond repair. Out of it tumbled a human race identical to the tiny mice we saw that afternoon. Both were blind, one physically and the other spiritually. Helpless and naked, we, like the infant mice, were incapable of finding a way out of the dilemma. Hope for the future required outside assistance. Eternal death was our destiny—unless God intervened.

My thoughts then shifted to a dark, foreboding hill on which three crosses were erected. There I saw God's own Son defeating the threats of Satan as He sacrificed His life for me. Superimposed upon this was the glorious sight of an empty tomb and the vision of a risen

Savior who is continually searching for the lost. Just like that valiant mother mouse, He is determined to continue through the leaves under which we attempt to hide until He finds that very last one of us. Waiting at the doorstep of a new shelter is a Father eager to welcome us to our eternal home.

My heart overflowed with gratitude at the realization that I was a member of the family of "the God who would not quit!" My God never gives up. He kept on searching until even I had been found and rescued. On that bright October afternoon, tears mingled with perspiration as I felt God's arms of love and compassion encompass me.

(Jesus said to him) *"For the Son of Man came to seek and to save what was lost."* Luke 19:10

You see, at just the right time, when we were still powerless, Christ died for the ungodly. Romans 5:6

This is good, and pleases God our Savior, who wants all men to be saved and to come to a knowledge of the truth. 1 Timothy 2:3–4

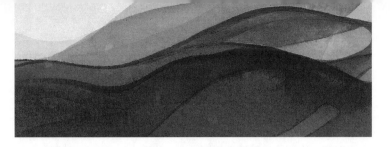

THE MIRACLE OF CHRISTMAS

The early morning Montana sun seared our bared brows as Lynn and I walked across the parking lot separating our motel from the nearby truck stop. It was the first indication of the oppressive heat that lay ahead.

A furtive movement that caught my eye midway across the softening asphalt interrupted our journey. Huddled in the protective shadow of a parked vehicle was a tiny white poodle. His blue knit sweater, designed to ward off the chill of the previous night, indicated that he was the prized possession of some proud owner. Troubled eyes following every movement, he took a few apprehensive steps in our direction. An extended hand of friendship, however, resulted in a hasty retreat to his self-designated shelter.

His vantage point not only offered welcome shade but also permitted unobstructed viewing of every vehicle that stopped for refueling. It initially appeared that he was awaiting the return of his owners from the near-by restaurant. Each alighting occupant was warily approached as the forlorn poodle searched for a familiar form and scent. Lack of recognition was followed by a dejected, head-hung-low return to his place of refuge.

A conversation with the restaurant cashier confirmed our assumption. The dog had been there since before daybreak, apparently inadvertently left behind by a traveler. It was easy to picture heartbroken family members who had discovered their loss and were now retracing steps in an attempt to locate a precious pet.

A waitress offered him a bowl of water and tender morsels of meat, but even pangs of hunger and thirst could not overcome his deep distrust. An attempt to pet him resulted in his headlong flight along the interstate.

Our concern for his safety and comfort increased as the hours went by. Sunlight had given way to dusk when, through our window, we saw a familiar white sweater-clad figure gingerly picking his way across the open field behind our motel. He cautiously approached the chain link enclosure of the kennel directly beneath our window and briefly touched noses with its single occupant.

We wanted to communicate with him, to assure him that we could help. But with heavy hearts we continued to watch our tiny friend return to his lonely vigil.

He eventually disappeared in the inky darkness and we never saw him again.

How similar the condition of that dog to the situation in which we find ourselves as we try to use our human form of reason to envision God. Our limited impressions of God are often formed by the things we see happening all around us.

"If God is supposed to be good," someone asks, "and He is in control, then why do I experience the deep distress in my life? Why is there so much pain and suffering? Doesn't He care about the breakup of families, the wars between nations, the death and starvation? If He is powerful, then He must also be cruel!"

It is this last impression that causes us to resent the thought of that kind of god intruding in our life. Just as with that tiny poodle, the vision of a god such as this approaching us with an upraised hand arouses fear and trembling deep within. Rather than drawing near in confidence we flee in terror.

The true God was aware of the instinctive distrust we inherited from Adam and Eve. He used the language of pictures to help us understand things beyond our limited grasp. But we are like the dog. Depending on our circumstances, the words can sound hollow and devoid of meaning.

God speaks of His love for us—but all we see is the

fickle nature of our self-centered human love that takes advantage of others. God refers to Himself as Father—but some have only experienced the shortcomings and failures of their own fathers. God promises to be with us always—while friends who have spoken similar words inflict unbearable pain. We paint our picture of God by referring to that which we saw around us.

What a gift of grace that God the Son, Jesus Christ, became one of us. He translated God's unintelligible words into a language we could understand. He revealed to us the true face of God.

"God does love you," our Savior said, "but it is different from the love you are accustomed to. It is a perfect love that expresses itself as a selfless concern for every individual, no matter what."

Our Lord continued beyond mere explanation. He lived that unconditional love. He offered living water to a woman who came to a well in Samaria. He had dinner with a sinful tax collector called Zacchaeus. He stretched out His hand to a woman caught in adultery. He shunned palaces of the powerful and lived among the poor and downtrodden. Ultimately He sacrificed His very life on a criminal's cross and rose again to prove the validity of His message. It was as if He said, "Yes, God is all-powerful, but His deepest desire is to use it on your behalf for your immediate and eternal welfare."

As Jesus walked through our world, He used the power in His touch to make the blind to see and the deaf to hear, the lame to walk and the broken heart whole. He forgave the sinner and raised the dead, even as He fed the multitudes and defeated Satan. Everything He did was on our behalf. He employed the power of our heavenly Father when He reconstructed the maimed lives of those He encountered. He refused to use this power to destroy, even when others pleaded with Him to do just that.

Those who lived with Him and walked at His side were bathed in the warmth of His presence and lost the fear they had inherited because of their sin. "Anyone who has seen Me has seen the Father," declared Jesus to His disciples. His followers came to understand that the upraised hands of God mean blessing and not punishment, that extended arms are there to protect and not to crush. Through the power of the Holy Spirit, the 33 years between the human birth and death of God's Son had their desired effect.

The testimonies of those who witnessed His deeds and lived in His presence have been preserved for you and me in the Bible. "God *is* love," John states with absolute assurance, and then fills the words with meaning by providing intimate insights into the teachings of our Messiah.

It was Jesus who knelt down and gently whispered

words in my language that brought me comfort and safety and the sure promise of forgiveness. It was Jesus who identified me as a redeemed child of God. And it was that same Jesus who, through His body and blood, restored me to my Father's arms where I now rest securely—and will for all eternity. That is the miracle of Christmas. It is my prayer that you have taken hold of this identical miracle in your own life.

The Word became flesh and made His dwelling among us. We have seen His glory, the glory of the One and Only, who came from the Father, full of grace and truth. John 1:14

"Anyone who has seen Me has seen the Father. How can you say, 'Show us the Father'? Don't you believe that I am in the Father, and that the Father is in Me? The words I say to you are not just My own. Rather, it is the Father, living in Me, who is doing His work." John 14:9b–10

HE PAID THE PRICE

The awesome and wonderful story of Christ's suffering and death is one you have heard many times. What would it have been like to actually have been there, to see, hear, and even participate in the events of that tragic week? We have the wonderful eyewitness accounts provided for us in God's Word that give evidence. But what if we witnessed such a sacrifice within the context of today?

Please indulge me as I share one perspective through this fictitious story. I hope it captures a tiny bit of what those who were there may have felt during those momentous days.

A number of years ago a man felt an intense desire to help people trapped by unfortunate circumstances. Therefore, he became involved in a prison ministry where he spent time with those awaiting execution. Several inmates began to trust him and shared intimate details of their earlier days.

One of the stories was so pathetic that it aroused his sympathy. It became apparent that inmate #2431, though now filled with hatred, might respond positively to counseling if enough time were available. Unfortunately, his execution date was six weeks away. So touched was the man, however, that saving this person from the death penalty became an all-consuming passion.

The judge who had imposed the sentence was contacted with the plea that a reprieve be granted—to no avail. The crime this man had committed was so heinous that commuting the sentence was unthinkable.

The man was sick at heart and filled with despair. His wife noticed his mood, and her questioning prompted him to explain. Their only son, Dave, sat at the dinner table with them. He listened intently as his father described the brutal child abuse to which this inmate had been subjected, and how he felt that the inmate deserved a second chance. This father's anger at the lack of response on the part of the judge was also shared.

The next morning Dave came to his father with a shocking request. "Dad," he said, "I also feel compassion for #2431. I realize that the judge cannot change the sentence because the laws of the state must be fulfilled. However, do you think he might grant a pardon if I were executed in place of the prisoner?"

Dave's proposal made the father recoil in horror. He wanted to drive the thought from his son's mind, despite his insistence that he was both willing and unafraid to die. A week was to go by before the father presented his plan to the judge.

The judge's initial hasty rejection was followed by a request for time to study the statutes pertaining to sentencing. His decision was announced 10 days later. "I find no law forbidding the execution of one person in the place of another," he declared. "Furthermore, a pardon will be offered the guilty party provided that the person who is executed in his place is innocent of all crimes. Your son appears to qualify, so the substitution is approved."

The execution date was one week away when Dave willingly entered the tiny cramped cell. His father's visits during the next six days were filled with the sharing of a deep love that flowed between them. The intense sorrow felt as the time for the ending of his son's life drew near was tempered by their mutual desire for the new life that #2431 would soon experience.

It is hard for the father to relive the last moments spent with his son on that final morning. They cried when they heard the footsteps of the executioner echoing in the hall. Final endearments were whispered as they clung to one another. Then the cell door opened, and a man entered to lead Dave to the death chamber. In that instant the father saw a trace of fear on his son's face.

"Dad," he pleaded, "please stay close to me. I want to see your face and be assured of your love as I die. Please, Dad, please walk beside me and hold my hand as I take my final steps!"

They walked out of the cell side by side, and started down the hall leading to the death chamber. At that point the father briefly looked into Dave's eyes, then wrenched his hand from his grasp and turned to walk in the opposite direction, never once looking back. Dave's cries for his father's return went unheeded. He had abandoned his son in his moment of greatest need, and left him to die alone.

"How horrible," you are probably saying to yourself, "how could anyone do something like that!" Yes, it is unthinkable. The very thought of walking away crushes my heart. Yet Scripture tells us that is exactly what God did as His Son hung on the cross. All the pain and terror of hell is expressed in that anguished cry, "My God, My God, why have You forsaken Me?" The Father turned His back on Jesus so you and I might never be separated from His presence. It was at that moment that your pardon was purchased, the cell door was opened, and you were set free.

Or don't you know that all of us who were baptized into Christ Jesus were baptized into His death? We were therefore buried with Him through baptism into death in order that, just as Christ was raised from the dead through the glory of the Father, we too may live a new life. Romans 6:3–4

But because of His great love for us, God, who is rich in mercy, made us alive with Christ even when we were dead in transgressions—it is by grace you have been saved. Ephesians 2:4–5

MATTER OF FAITH

Webster's *Seventh New Collegiate Dictionary* defines faith as "belief and trust in and loyalty to God, ... firm belief in something for which there is no proof."

Hebrews 11, that great faith chapter, begins by stating, "Now faith is being sure of what we hope for and certain of what we do not see" (Hebrews 11:1).

Faith may appear to be cloaked in mystery—until we begin to realize the role it plays in our day-to-day living. We all demonstrate faith in the mechanical reliability of the steering mechanism, for example, of the cars we drive as we twist our way through heavy traffic. We wait until the last possible second before applying the brakes because of our faith in the dependability of the braking system.

E-mail messages are transmitted and received with confidence although few of us understand the enabling microchip circuitry. Few qualms are experienced when boarding a passenger jet and quickly ascending to a cruise altitude of six miles. Yet the exact nature of gravity, one of the forces that interact to make flight possible, still remains a mystery. Even scientists who accept as true only that which is verifiable must, at the same time, admit to faith in the unchangeable characteristics of the forces of nature.

Once explained, the secular faith we exhibit every day is easier to comprehend. But what about religious faith? What is it? Where does it come from? How does it become ours? These are bewildering questions that can lead to anxiety and lack of assurance.

I once saw a bumper sticker that attempted to convey the simple spiritual message "Faith Saves!" It sounded so biblical, so confident, and so Christian. Yet it was so wrong. Those two words indicate that you and I are saved because of our faith. That concept transforms faith into a work that we must perform in order to earn our salvation. If we accept this ground rule, then we are left with a troubling question: "Is my faith strong enough to save me?" That question can never be answered, and we are left with only doubt.

In truth, it is not our faith, but the *object* of our faith, which guarantees our salvation. When Christ cried out, "It is finished!" He was telling us that our redemption was assured. Christ had paid the full penalty demanded by God. He had suffered the torment of hell as our substitute. He had endured the bitter anguish of total separation from His Father. The complete ransom had been paid. There was, and is, nothing left for us to do.

It was as though an innocent person had been convicted by a judge and then executed as a substitute for a convicted criminal. Following his death the judge decided that the sacrifice of this one individual paid for all the penalties of all the other men on death row. "Justice has been satisfied," he declared. "I am issuing a pardon for each and every person imprisoned and awaiting executing. They are now innocent in the eyes of the law!"

That is exactly what God has done. He has declared that all people are now justified in His sight. This is what is meant when we are told in 2 Corinthians 5:19 "that God was reconciling the world to Himself in Christ, not counting men's sins against them." We are righteous because God has declared us to be so, not because of anything we have done. The payment made by His Son has satisfied God's requirement for justice.

"God so loved the world, ..." we are told in John 3:16. St. Paul summarizes it beautifully in Romans 3:23–24, "for all have sinned and fall short of the glory of God, and are justified freely by His grace through the redemption that came by Christ Jesus."

"God so loved the world," "all have sinned," "and [all] are justified." God has prepared a pardon for and offers it to every individual who ever has lived, is living, or is awaiting birth. But we have also been created with a free will. God's gift of grace and pardon can either be accepted by faith or rejected.

It is at this point where it becomes easy for the mind to rebel. Our logic seems to tell us that, since all have been declared justified, then all should be saved. After all, didn't Christ make the total payment for the entire world? Why then is it necessary to personally receive this pardon, using faith as the vehicle? A personal experience has helped me to understand.

Long ago, polio epidemics left sorrowing families of those who either died or were handicapped. A man working beside me in an air conditioning factory contracted the disease and died several days later, leaving behind a grieving widow and two small children.

Lynn and I anxiously watched our four children during summer months, looking for the telltale signs indicating that the virus had struck. Public gatherings were shunned, since this was thought to be where the polio virus could be communicated. Prevention appeared to be impossible and cures were infrequent. The arrival of fall was always accompanied by a gigantic nationwide sigh of relief.

Finally the prayers of a nation were answered. In 1953, a research team headed by Dr. Jonas Salk discovered a vaccine that they felt would prevent the disease. Our oldest daughter was one of a number of school children selected to participate in a blind study designed to prove the effectiveness of the medical discovery. Half the children were injected with the vaccine, while the other half received a saline solution. By the end of the summer the results indicated that the vaccine both prevented polio and could be administered safely.

A way had been found to eliminate the fear of polio. Within months enough vaccine had been manufactured to provide protection for all the people of our nation. My wife and I had faith in the stamp of approval given by both the medical profession and federal government and all the members of our family were vaccinated. What a relief to know that we were now protected from the disease and need no longer live in fear of what summer would bring.

At the same time there were parents who exercised their freedom by refusing to have their children vaccinated. Some did it because of personal beliefs. Others lacked faith in the product. There was an additional group who somehow failed to learn of this discovery and its availability.

The end of 1955 arrived with a large number of children still unprotected. Some contracted polio and a small percentage of that number died. The vaccine had been discovered, perfected, and made available to all.

Yet it failed to prevent the disease in those particular children because they had not received it personally.

It is in a similar way that Christ has provided the means whereby our eternal death can be prevented. It is a "vaccine" offered in unlimited quantity and available to all people. However, just as parents could make a conscious decision to reject the polio vaccine, so our free will can also lead us to reject what God offers.

But there is a major difference between these scenarios. Only a small percentage of those who rejected the offer to be vaccinated contracted polio, and of that group a lesser number died. Christ's atonement for our sins differs in that it is absolute. Those who accept and cling to it will live eternally, while everyone who rejects it will suffer the torment of everlasting separation from God.

Consider this: What was it that averted the disease? Was it the act of faith or the vaccine itself? The answer is rather obvious. Although Lynn and I had faith in the reliability of the product and the competence of the research team, that was not enough to protect our children. Their safety was assured only after the vaccine had been injected. It was not our faith, but rather the object of our faith that brought a prayer of thanksgiving to our lips.

Just so it is with the pardon, or reconciliation,

which is offered by God. It is Christ's payment that has earned for us the gift of eternal life. Faith is the "needle" through which this reconciliation becomes ours. The Holy Spirit uses both Word and Sacrament to create this "needle" that brings faith in the redeeming work of Christ in our lives. I *know* it is present in my heart. Is it present in yours?

SHADOW

Neighborhood cats have always loved our backyard. A graceful leap over a weathered three-foot fence takes them to our grassy plot. There they crouch in various attitudes of expectation. Seemingly hypnotized by the comings and goings of the finches, sparrows, jays, and others seeking repast at feeders and water basins, they invariably succumb to patient (and usually futile) feline musings.

All but one have aroused my ire as they blatantly stalk the objects of my affection. The daily visits of the one exception commenced one spring. A pale fawn coat, dark tail, and eyes of robin's-egg blue bespoke the royal line of the Siamese. Her beauty was obvious. However, it was a shy demeanor in marked contrast to the strutting haughtiness of her fellow intruders that drew my attention and presented a personal challenge.

Within weeks, I found myself engaged in a struggle

to win her confidence. The wall of separation was well defined and seemingly impenetrable. Distrust of any human was apparent. An image in a window drew instant fear. The sudden opening of a door prompted headlong flight. Hunting forays were limited to the perimeters where her progress from bush to bush so resembled a shadow that it became the name by which she was affectionately known.

The plan that gradually evolved required the utmost in patience. The initial step concentrated on moderating her instinct for flight by silently standing beside the back door. As the weeks went by, she reluctantly began to accept my presence. She also became accustomed to the sound of my voice as I softly called "Shadow." The slightest movement in her direction, however, would trigger a hasty departure.

I wish it were possible to report that all my plotting and planning has led to unmitigated success, and that today a trusting and loving Shadow greets me by rubbing her body against my leg. Unfortunately, that is far from the truth. Efforts were intensified that summer after her return from an unexplained three-month absence. Daily portions of choice tidbits were introduced in an attempt to convince her that I was an okay kind of guy. Long periods were spent using all the persuasive powers I could muster to communicate both my admiration and concern for her. All was for naught. She would not let me enter her 20-

foot comfort zone.

Two things finally became apparent. First, no matter how gentle and well-spoken, words alone were incapable of crushing the barrier that stood between us. It would take the touch of my hand to finally subdue her instinctive fear. Second, achieving that goal would require getting down to her level. My upright figure would always be threatening from her perspective.

Late in fall our neighbors witnessed an unusual spectacle. I wonder what thoughts crossed their minds as they saw a white-haired man crawling across the yard on his hands and knees whispering, "Shadow is a pretty kitty." My slow and cautious crawl enabled me to approach within five feet before Shadow's anxiety became apparent. Plans to repeat the procedure the following day were foiled, however, when my tawny friend failed to appear. I have not seen her since. Perhaps she is off on another extended visit to "the far country." Wherever she may be, I am anxiously awaiting her return. There is seldom a morning that goes by without my wondering if this will finally be the day when I reach out and touch my feline friend.

Was the crawl worth the effort? To an outsider the obvious answer is no. "Why humiliate yourself," they might say, "to win the affection of a lowly cat?" But for me it was a memorable moment, an initial step in satisfying a yearning to forge a bond with this beautiful creature.

I began to wonder how similar this was to our own situation with God.

Today, in reflection, I can see the similarity between Shadow and mankind's situation with God. However, instead of months it took thousands of years for the world to fully grasp God's plan to destroy the inherited barrier separating us from Him. God spoke words to allay human fears, but like the cat, even words gently spoken could not be understood.

But when the time was fully come, God did the unthinkable. He descended to our level, crawling on hands and knees across the hills of Judea to a humble stable in Bethlehem. For that tiny baby cradled in a manger, it was the beginning of a lifelong effort to reach out and touch us.

Thirty-three years, the length of a painful journey that began in a stable, led to a cross, and culminated in an open tomb. Fortunately it has not yet ended. He still walks beside us, our Savior at our side, reaching out to those struggling to overcome an inherited fear born of sin. But forgiveness and mercy are ours. It comes to us because of a Father's grace that we receive through Word and Sacrament. Today Christ's hand stretches out to offer each one of us the grace and mercy of a Father who loves us. Will you receive His gift so freely offered? It is there, just as it once was for Shadow.

In [Jesus] we have redemption through His blood, the forgiveness of sins, in accordance with the riches of God's grace that He lavished on us with all wisdom and understanding. Ephesians 1:7–8

AUTHOR BIOGRAPHY

Dick Korthals has 30 years of experience as a leader of spiritual growth seminars and retreats and is a frequent speaker at special events. Following his retirement from the Air Force, where he was a pilot, engineer, and professor, Korthals was university professor and administrator. The author of *Reach Out* and *Agape Evangelism*, as well as dozens of articles and stories, he is a lay minister and writer for Focus on the Family.